DK *Mini Makes*

CROCHET

MORE THAN 30 HANDMADE GIFTS TO GIVE

 Penguin
Random
House

Project Editor Elizabeth Yeates
Designer Alison Gardner
Jacket Design Alison Gardner
Pre-Production Producer David Almond
Producer Denitsa Kenanska
Special Sales Creative Project Manager
Alison Donovan

First published in Great Britain in 2015
by Dorling Kindersley Limited,
80 Strand, London WC2R 0RL

Material previously published in
Crochet (2014)

A CIP catalogue record for this book
is available from the British Library
ISBN 978-0-2414-5978-2

Printed and bound in China

All images © Dorling Kindersley Limited
For further information see: **www.dkimages.com**

A WORLD OF IDEAS:
SEE ALL THERE IS TO KNOW

www.dk.com

Contents

Introduction

This book is suitable for all crocheters – beginners with no previous experience, and those with more advanced skills. If you have never held a crochet hook before, but want to learn, this book will take you through all the basic crochet stitches to enable you to make beautiful items. If you already know how to crochet, you will find a wonderful collection of unique and attractive, good-value patterns to try out.

Mini Makes Crochet guides you through the basic techniques and stitches – presented clearly and simply with step-by-step photographs – covering the relevant abbreviations and symbols on the way. Beginners can work through the comprehensive and easy-to-follow techniques section in the first part of the book, stopping along the way to try out a mini project to practise the stitch they have just learned. More experienced crocheters can dip into this section to revisit stitches they already know. The mini projects include items ranging from washcloths (pp.60-61) made using double crochet to a stylish intarsia cushion (pp.76-77).

Once you are confident with all the crochet stitches, you can launch into the projects chapter, and begin making crocheted items as diverse as a chunky socks (pp104-105), a tiny flower pin cushion (pp.68-69), and a little girl's summer tunic dress (pp.114-115).

With more than 30 projects to choose from, there is something for everyone: from rugs and cushions, to hats and scarves; gloves, socks, and slippers; garments and bags; plus charming toys to make. *Mini Makes Crochet* will enable you to make your own unique, bespoke crocheted pieces for yourself, your home, and your family and friends.

Techniques

Basic stitches

Learning to crochet can take a bit of time because there are several basic stitches to master. But there is no need to learn all the stitches at once. With only chain stitches and double crochet at your disposal, you can make attractive striped blankets and cushion covers in luscious yarns.

Getting started

Before making your first loop, the slip knot (see opposite), get to know the hook and how to hold it. Then try out the various hook- and yarn-holding techniques (below), when learning how to make chain stitches. If you ever learned crochet as a child, you will automatically hold the hook the way you originally learned to, and you should stick to this whether it is the pencil or knife position.

Holding the hook

Left-handed crocheters hold the hook in the exact mirror image of right-handed crocheters

Left-handed crocheters hold the hook in the exact mirror image of right-handed crocheters

Pencil position: To hold the hook in this position, grip it as you would a pencil. If the hook has a shaped thumb rest, position this above your thumb and under your forefinger. The centre of your thumb will be about 5cm (2in) from the tip of the hook if the hook has a thumb rest, and this is where you should also hold a hook without a thumb rest.

Knife position: To hold a crochet hook in this position, grip it as you would when using a table knife to cut food. As for the pencil position, if the hook has a thumb rest, settle your thumb and forefinger in this shaped section with the centre of your thumb about 5cm (2in) from the hook tip. Grip a hook without a thumb rest the same distance from the tip.

Holding the yarn

In order to control the flow of the yarn to your hook, you need to lace it around the fingers of your free hand (called your yarn hand). Both the techniques shown here are only suggestions, so feel free to develop your own.

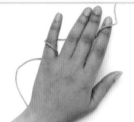

Left-handed crocheters thread the yarn through their right hand

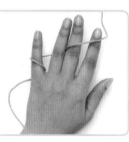

Left-handed crocheters thread the yarn through their right hand

Method one: Start by winding the yarn around your little finger, then pass it under your two middle fingers and over your forefinger. With this method the forefinger is used to position the yarn.

Method two: Wrap the yarn around your little finger, then pass it behind the next finger and over the top of the middle finger and forefinger. This method allows you to position the yarn with either the forefinger or middle finger, whichever is more comfortable and gives you more control (see Tensioning your yarn, opposite).

Making a slip knot

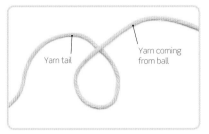

Yarn tail

Yarn coming from ball

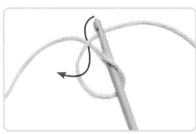

1 To make the first loop (called the slip knot) on your hook, begin by crossing the yarn coming from the ball over the yarn end (called the yarn tail) to form a circle of yarn.

2 Insert the tip of the hook through the circle of yarn. Then use the hook to grab the ball end of the yarn and pull the yarn through the circle.

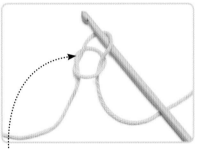

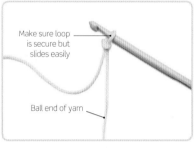

Make sure loop is secure but slides easily

Ball end of yarn

3 This forms a loop on the hook and a loose, open knot below the loop.

4 Pull both ends of the yarn firmly to tighten the knot and the loop around the shank of the hook.

5 Make sure the completed slip knot is tight enough on the hook so that it won't fall off, but not so tight that you can barely slide it along the hook's shank. The yarn tail on the slip knot should be at least 10cm (4in) long so it can be darned in later.

Tensioning your yarn

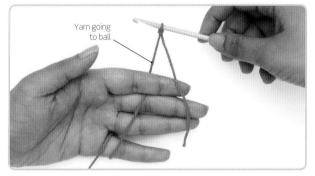

Yarn going to ball

Hold your crochet firmly close to the hook

Yarn going to ball

1 With your slip knot on your hook, try out some yarn-holding techniques. Wrap the yarn around your little finger and then lace it through your other fingers as desired, but so that it ends up over the tip of your forefinger (or your forefinger and middle finger).

2 As you crochet, grip the yarn tightly with your little finger and ring finger and release it gently as you form the loops. Use either your forefinger or your middle finger to position the yarn, and hold the base of the crochet close to the hook to keep it in place as the hook is drawn through the loops.

Chain stitches (Abbreviation = ch)

Chain stitches are the first crochet stitches you need to learn because they form the base for all other stitches – called a foundation chain – and for turning chains. They are used in combination with other basic stitches to create a vast array of crochet stitch patterns, both densely textured stitches and lacy ones. Practise chain stitches until you are comfortable holding a hook and releasing and tensioning yarn.

Making a foundation chain

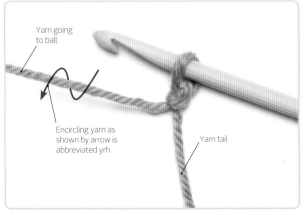

Yarn going to ball

Encircling yarn as shown by arrow is abbreviated yrh

Yarn tail

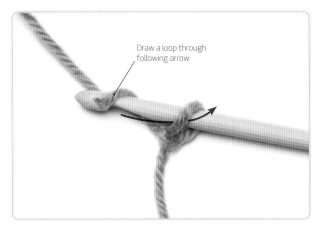

Draw a loop through following arrow

1 Start with a slip knot on your hook (see p.9). Wrap the yarn around the hook; this action is called "yarn round hook" (abbreviated yrh) in crochet patterns. When working a yrh, move your hook under the yarn at the same time as you move the yarn slightly forwards.

2 With the yarn gripped in the lip of the hook, draw a loop of yarn through the loop on the hook. (Hold the base of the slip knot with the free fingers of your yarn hand as you draw the loop through.)

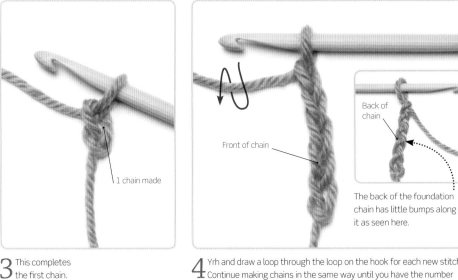

1 chain made

Front of chain

Back of chain

The back of the foundation chain has little bumps along it as seen here.

3 This completes the first chain.

4 Yrh and draw a loop through the loop on the hook for each new stitch. Continue making chains in the same way until you have the number specified in your crochet pattern.

Counting chain stitches

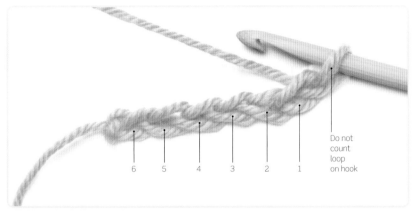

6 5 4 3 2 1 Do not count loop on hook

Counting correctly: As you make chains for the foundation chain, count each stitch until you have made the required number. Then before starting your crochet, recount the chains to check that you have the correct number. With the front of the chain facing you, start counting the stitches from the base of your hook and count leftwards.

Fastening off chains and slip stitches

Stopping your crochet when it is complete is called fastening off. As there is only one loop on your hook, the process is extremely simple. Here is a visual aid for how to fasten off a length of chains or a row of slip stitches. The principle is the same for all stitches in crochet.

Fastening off a length of chains

1 Remove the loop from the hook. Pull out the loop to enlarge it so that it does not start to unravel.

2 Cut the yarn, pass the cut yarn end through the loop, and pull tight to close the loop. Make sure you leave a long enough yarn end to darn invisibly into the chain later, if necessary.

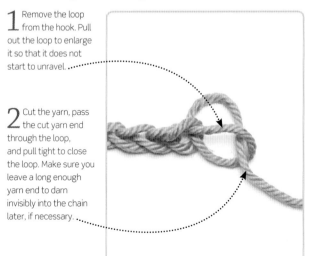

Fastening off slip stitches

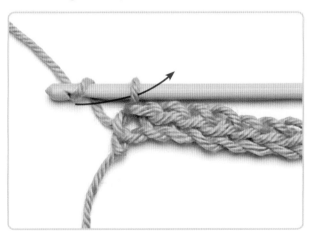

Securing ends: Fasten off in the same way as for the chain stitches. Alternatively, you can use the hook to draw the cut end through the remaining loop as shown here by the large arrow.

Slip stitch (Abbreviation = ss)

Slip stitches are the shortest of all the crochet stitches. Although they can be worked in rows, the resulting fabric is so dense that it is only really suitable for bag handles. However, slip stitches appear very frequently in crochet instructions – to join on new yarn (see p.17), to work invisibly along the top of a row to move to a new position (see p.25), and to join rounds in circular crochet – making them one of the most useful stitches of all.

Working slip stitch as a fabric

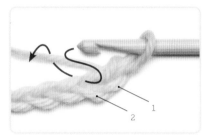

1 Make a foundation chain of the required length. To begin the first stitch, insert the hook through the second chain from the hook, passing the hook under only one strand of the chain. Then wrap the yarn around the hook (yrh).

2 Holding the base of the chain firmly with the fingers of your left hand and tensioning the yarn (see p.9), draw a loop back through the chain and through the loop on the hook as shown by the large arrow.

3 Continue across the foundation chain, working a slip stitch into each chain in the same way. Always work slip stitches fairly loosely for whatever purpose you are using them.

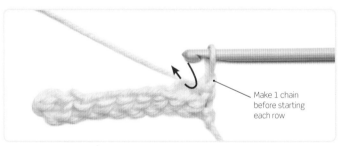

Make 1 chain before starting each row

4 After the last stitch of the row has been completed, and if you want to work another row, turn your crochet to position the yarn at the right edge of the piece of crochet ready to begin the second row.

5 To begin a second row of slip stitches, make one chain stitch. This chain is called the turning chain. For the second and following rows of slip stitch, work each stitch into the back loop only of the top of the stitches below. (It is not essential for a beginner to practise working slip stitch in rows as it is rarely used this way.)

Using slip stitches to form a foundation ring

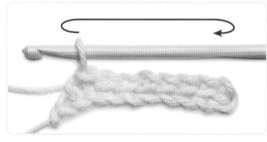

Making a ring: Slip stitches are also used to form the foundation rings for circular crochet (see p.46). Make the required number of chains for the ring, then insert the hook through the first chain made, wrap the yarn around the hook, and draw a loop through the chain and the loop on the hook to close the ring.

These motifs are formed by first making a
foundation ring. The technique (left), only
requires basic crochet stitches. Joined motifs
are great for making small items, such as bags or
cushion covers, but also for scarves and shawls,
especially when made in gossamer mohair.

Double crochet (Abbreviation = dc)

Double crochet is the easiest crochet stitch to learn and one crocheters use most frequently, either on its own or in combination with other stitches. Take your time learning and practising the stitch because once you become proficient, the taller stitches will be much easier to master. Double crochet forms a dense fabric that is suitable for many types of garments and accessories. It is also the stitch used for toys and containers because it can be worked very tightly to form a stiff, firm textile that has excellent rigidity, prevents toy stuffing from showing through the stitches, and holds up well.

Working in rows: When double crochet is worked back and forth in rows, it looks identical on both sides. Worked in the round it looks different on the right and wrong sides, which you can see on p.46.

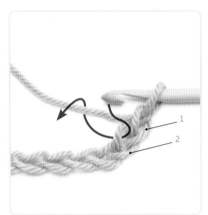

1 Make a foundation chain of the required length (see p.10). Insert the hook through the second stitch from the hook and wrap the yarn around the hook (yrh) following the large arrow. (You can insert the hook under one or two strands of the chain, but working under just one loop as shown here is easiest.)

2 Holding the base of the chain firmly with your left hand and tensioning the yarn (see p.9), draw a loop back through the chain as shown by the large arrow.

3 There are now 2 loops on the hook. Next, yrh as shown by the large arrow.

4 Draw a loop through both loops on the hook in one smooth action. As you use the yarn, allow it to flow through the fingers of your left hand while still tensioning it softly.

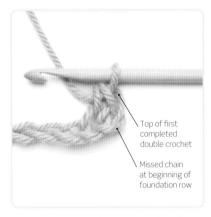

Top of first completed double crochet

Missed chain at beginning of foundation row

5 This completes the first double crochet. The missed chain at the beginning of this first row does NOT count as a stitch on its own (in other words, it is not counted when you count how many stitches are in the row and it is not worked into in the next row).

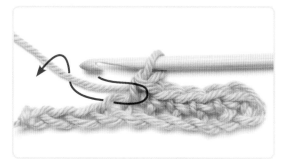

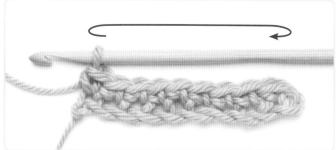

6 Continue across the foundation chain, working one double crochet into each chain in the same way.

7 At the end of the row, turn your crochet to position the yarn at the right edge of the piece of crochet, ready to begin the second row.

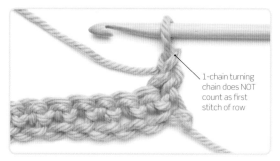

1-chain turning chain does NOT count as first stitch of row

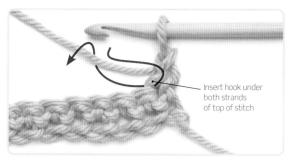

Insert hook under both strands of top of stitch

8 To begin the second row, make one chain stitch. This chain is called the turning chain, and it brings the work up to the height of the double crochet stitches that will follow.

9 Work the first double crochet into the top of the first stitch in the row below. Be sure to insert the hook under both legs of the "V" of the stitch. Work a double crochet into the top of each of the remaining double crochets in the row below.

10 At the end of the row, work the last stitch into the top of the last double crochet of the row below. Work following rows as for the second row.

11 When you have completed your crochet, cut the yarn leaving a long loose end – at least 10cm (4in) long. Remove the hook from the remaining loop, pass the yarn end through the loop, and pull tight to close it. Fastening off like this is applicable for all crochet stitches.

Half treble crochet (Abbreviation = htr)

After double crochet, half treble crochet comes next in order of stitch heights (see p.30). It is firm like double crochet and fairly dense, but produces a slightly softer texture, which makes it ideal for warm baby garments. The texture is also more interesting than double crochet, but not too lacy. It's not advisable to move on to learning how to work half trebles until you can make double crochet stitches with confidence.

Working in rows: Half treble crochet worked in rows, as here, looks the same on both sides, making it a totally reversible fabric, just like all basic stitches worked in rows.

1 Make a foundation chain of the required length (see p.10). To begin the first stitch, wrap the yarn around the hook (yrh).

2 Insert the hook through the third chain from the hook, yrh again (as shown by the large arrow), and draw a loop back through the chain.

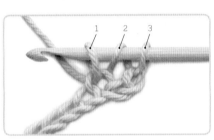

3 There are now 3 loops on the hook.

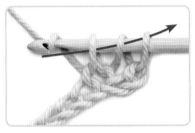

4 Yrh and draw a loop through all 3 loops on the hook as shown by the large arrow. (This motion becomes more fluid with practice.)

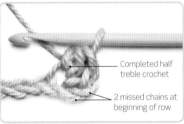

Completed half treble crochet

2 missed chains at beginning of row

5 This completes the first half treble.

6 Work one half treble crochet into each chain in the same way. Remember to start each half treble by wrapping the yarn around the hook before inserting it through the chain.

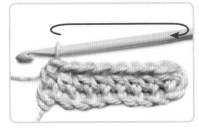

7 After working a half treble crochet into the last chain, turn the work to position the yarn at the right edge of the piece of crochet ready to begin the second row.

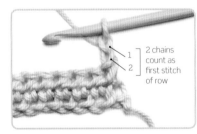
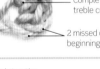

2 chains count as first stitch of row

8 Begin the second row by making 2 chains. This turning chain brings the work up to the height of the half trebles that follow.

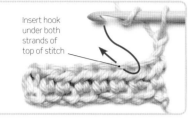

9 Yrh and work the first half treble into the top of the second stitch in the row below.

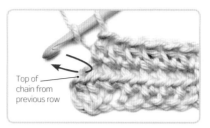

Top of chain from previous row

10 Work a half treble into each of the remaining half treble crochets in the row below. Work the following rows as for the second row.

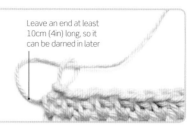

Leave an end at least 10cm (4in) long, so it can be darned in later

11 When the crochet is complete, cut the yarn. Remove the hook from the remaining loop, pass the yarn end through the loop, and pull tight to close the loop and fasten off securely.

Joining on new yarn

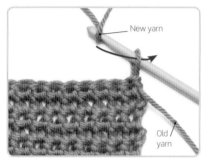

New yarn

Old yarn

Method one: Always join on a new yarn at the beginning of a row if possible. Simply drop the old yarn and pull the new yarn through the loop on the hook, then begin the row in the usual way. Darn in the yarn ends later.

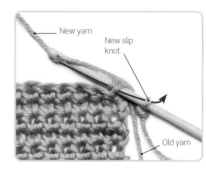

New yarn

New slip knot

Old yarn

Method two: This method is suitable for both stripes and plain crochet fabrics. First, fasten off the old yarn. Then place a slip knot on the hook, insert the hook through the first stitch of the row and draw a loop through the top of the stitch and the loop on the hook.

Simple stripes

Stripes worked in basic stitches have more potential for creativity than most crocheters realize. The only techniques you need to learn are how and when to change colours to start a new stripe, and how to carry the yarns up the side edge of the crochet.

Changing colours

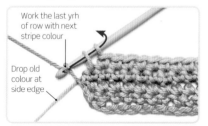

Work the last yrh of row with next stripe colour

Drop old colour at side edge

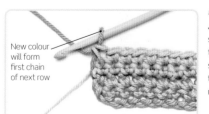

New colour will form first chain of next row

1 When working stripes in any stitch, always change to the next colour on the last yrh of the last row before the next stripe colour is started.

2 Drawing through the last yrh of the row completes the last stitch. The new colour is now on the hook ready to start the next stripe on the next row; this is so that the first turning chain in the next stripe is in the correct colour.

Carrying colours up side edge

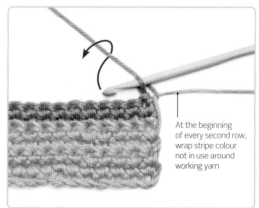

At the beginning of every second row, wrap stripe colour not in use around working yarn

Wrapping yarn: If a colour is not needed for more than 2 rows, wrap it around the other colour to secure it. If it is not needed for more than 8 rows, cut it off and rejoin it later.

Treble crochet (Abbreviation = tr)

Treble crochet produces a more open and softer crochet fabric than the denser double and half treble crochet. Because treble crochet is a tall stitch, the fabric grows quickly as you proceed, which makes it the most popular of all crochet stitches for projects that work up quickly.

Working in rows: As you work treble crochet in rows, you will see that it looks identical on the front and the back.

Make foundation chain of any length to practise trebles

1 Make as many chains as required. To begin the first stitch, wrap the yarn around the hook (yrh).

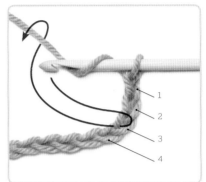

2 Insert the hook through the fourth chain from the hook, yrh again (as shown by the large arrow), and draw a loop back through the chain.

3 There are now 3 loops on the hook.

4 Yrh and draw a loop through the first 2 loops on the hook.

5 There are now 2 loops left on the hook. Yrh and draw a loop through the remaining 2 loops.

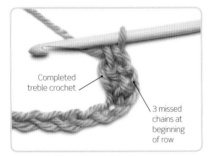

Completed treble crochet

3 missed chains at beginning of row

6 This completes the first treble. In treble crochet, the 3 missed chains at the beginning of the chain count as the first stitch of the foundation row.

7 Work one treble crochet into each chain in the same way. Remember to start each stitch with a yrh before inserting the hook through the chain.

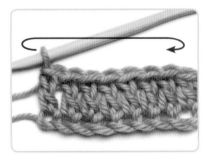

8 After the last stitch of the row has been completed, turn the work to position the yarn at the right edge of the piece of crochet ready to begin the second row.

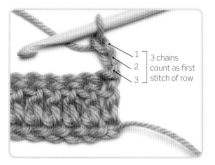

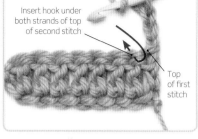

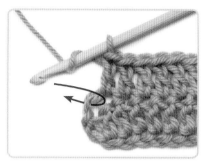

9 To begin the second row of treble crochet, make 3 chain stitches. This brings the work up to the height of these tall stitches.

10 Yrh, then, missing the first treble in the row below, work the first treble into the top of the second stitch.

Insert hook under both strands of top of second stitch

Top of first stitch

11 Work a treble into each stitch, working the last stitch into the top of the 3 chains. Work the following rows in the same way.

Counting crochet stitches

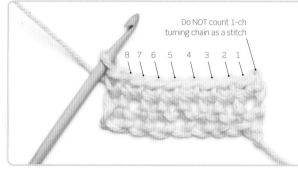

Do NOT count 1-ch turning chain as a stitch

8 7 6 5 4 3 2 1

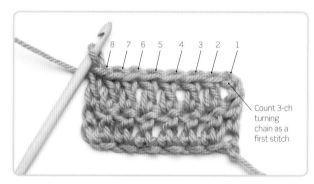

8 7 6 5 4 3 2 1

Count 3-ch turning chain as a first stitch

Counting double crochet stitches: With the front of the last row facing, count the top of each stitch. If you are losing stitches as your crochet grows, then you are probably failing to work into the last stitch in the row below; if you are gaining stitches, you may have worked twice into the same stitch.

Counting trebles: With the front of the last row facing, count the turning chain as the first stitch, then count the top of each treble. If you are losing stitches as your crochet grows, you are probably failing to work into the top of the turning chain; if you are gaining stitches, you may be working into the first treble of the row, instead of missing it.

Darning in yarn

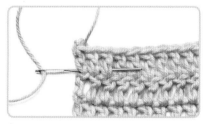

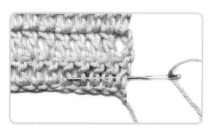

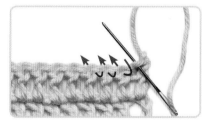

Darning in along top row: Using a blunt-ended yarn needle, darn the yarn end through the centre of the base of 6-8 stitches in the last row. Clip off the remaining end close to the fabric.

Darning in along first row: Using a blunt-ended yarn needle, darn the yarn end through the centre of the base of 6-8 stitches in the first row. Clip off the remaining end close to the fabric.

Darning in along top: You can also weave the yarn in and out of the top of the crochet. This provides a slightly more secure finishing and is good for slippery yarns.

Double treble crochet (Abbreviation = dtr)

Worked in a very similar way to treble crochet, double treble crochet stitches are approximately one chain length taller because the stitch is begun by wrapping the yarn around the hook twice instead of only once (see p.31).

Double trebles are often used in lace crochet (see pp.50-51), in crochet motifs, and in other fine cotton crochet patterns that require an open-textured result.

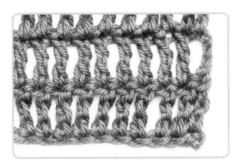

Double treble stitch: Producing a double-sided fabric, either side can be used as the right side. This stitch worked in rows grows quickly because the stitches are taller but not that much slower to work.

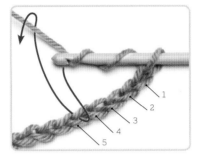

1 Make a foundation chain, then wrap the yarn twice around the hook (yrh) and insert the hook through the fifth chain from the hook.

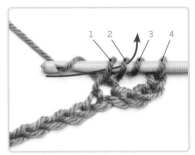

2 Yrh and draw a loop through the chain. There are now 4 loops on the hook. Yrh and draw a loop through the first 2 loops on the hook.

3 There are now 3 loops remaining. Yrh and draw a loop through the next 2 loops on the hook.

4 There are 2 loops remaining. Yrh and draw a loop through these final 2 loops.

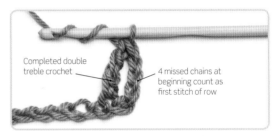

Completed double treble crochet

4 missed chains at beginning count as first stitch of row

5 This completes the first double treble. As for all tall crochet stitches, the missed chain stitches at the beginning of the foundation chain count as the first stitch of the foundation row.

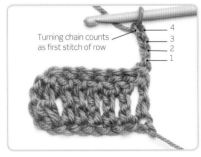

Turning chain counts as first stitch of row

6 Work one double treble into each chain in the same way. Then turn the crochet and begin the second row with a 4-chain turning chain.

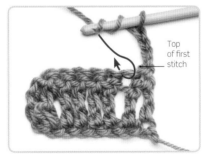

Top of first stitch

7 Miss the top of the first double treble in the row below and work the first double treble into the top of the second stitch.

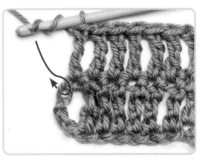

8 Work a double treble into each of the remaining double trebles in the row below. Work the last stitch of the row into the top of the 4 chains. Work following rows as for the second row.

Triple treble crochet (Abbreviation = trtr)

Stitches taller than double trebles are all worked in the same way as double trebles, except that the yarn is wrapped around the hook more times before the stitch is begun and they require taller turning chains. Once you have practised triple trebles and can work these easily, you will also be able to work quadruple and quintuple trebles without much effort. Triple treble stitch is a useful addition to your crochet repertoire.

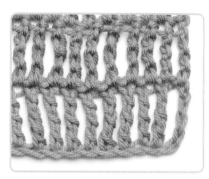

Triple treble stitch: This stitch worked in rows looks the same on both sides of the fabric. Notice how airy the crochet texture becomes as the basic stitches get taller.

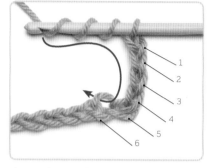

1 Wrap the yarn 3 times around the hook and insert the hook through the sixth stitch from the hook.

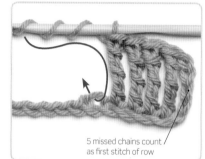

5 missed chains count as first stitch of row

2 Work the loops off the hook two at a time as for double trebles. Remember to wrap the yarn three times around the hook before starting each stitch. Start following rows with 5 chains.

Quadruple treble crochet (Abbreviation = qtr)

This stitch works in the same way as triple treble, except that the yarn is wound round the hook 4 times, and the hook is then inserted into the seventh stitch from the hook. The loops are then worked off two at a time, and following rows start with 6 chains.

Quadruple treble stitch: This stitch is noticeably taller than triple treble and also looks the same on both sides.

1 Once you know how to work the triple treble stitch, you can begin to see how each following stitch is worked. So, as a double treble wraps the yarn round the hook twice, so a triple treble wraps the yarn around 3 times. Therefore, a quadruple treble means you wrap the yarn around 4 times, and so on.

2 You work the loops off the hook in the same way as the double and triple treble, in pairs, until there is only the working loop left. Now you know the pattern, you can create a stitch as tall as you like.

Stitch heights

Each of the next stitches gets taller progressively and is worked by wrapping the yarn around the hook once more than the previous stitch, before inserting the hook. See page 30 for a diagram with basic stitch symbols.

Quintuple treble
Quadruple treble
Triple treble
Double treble
Treble
Half treble
Double

Shaping crochet

To progress from making simple squares and rectangles, a crocheter needs to know how to increase and decrease the number of stitches in the row to make shaped pieces of crocheted fabric. The most commonly used simple shaping techniques are illustrated in detail below.

Double crochet increases

Paired increases: Increases on garment pieces are most frequently worked as "paired increases" – an increase of one stitch at the beginning of the row and one at the end.

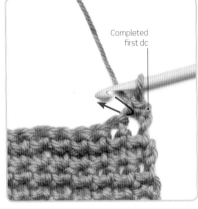

Completed first dc

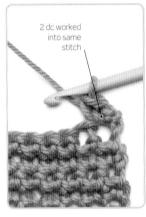

2 dc worked into same stitch

Completed first dc in last stitch

3 At the end of the row, work 1 dc into the last dc of the row in the usual way. Insert the hook again into the last dc of the row and work a second dc into it.

2 dc worked into same stitch

1 To increase one stitch at the beginning of a row of double crochet, work 1 dc into the first dc in the usual way. Next, insert the hook again into the first dc and work a second dc in the same stitch.

2 This completes the increase. Continue across the row, working 1 dc into each dc in the usual way.

4 This increases one stitch at the end of the row.

Treble crochet increases

End of row: Increases on garment pieces made using treble crochet are worked using the same techniques as for double crochet. Again, these increases are most frequently worked as "paired increases" – one stitch is increased at each end of the row.

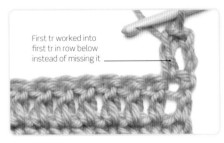

First tr worked into first tr in row below instead of missing it

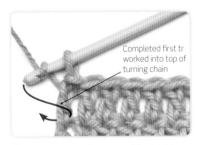

Completed first tr worked into top of turning chain

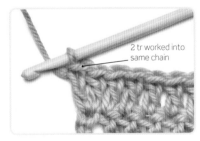

2 tr worked into same chain

1 To increase one stitch at the beginning of a row of treble crochet, first work the turning chain, then work 1 tr into the first tr in the row below. Because the first treble in the row below is usually missed, this creates an increase at the beginning of the row.

2 Continue across the row, working 1 tr into each tr in the usual way. At the end of the row, work 1 tr into the top of the turning chain in the row below in the usual way. Then work a second tr into the same turning chain.

3 This completes the one stitch increase at the end of the row as shown.

Step increase at beginning of row

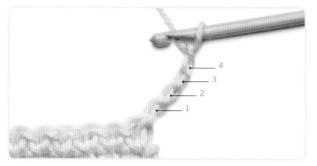

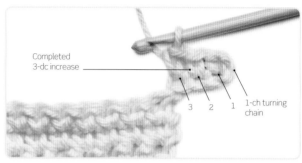

Completed
3-dc increase

3 2 1

1-ch turning
chain

1 Increases are also frequently worked in crochet so that they form little steps at the edge. As an example, to add a 3-stitch step increase at the beginning of a row of double crochet, begin by making 4 chains as shown here. (Always make one chain more than the number of extra double crochets required.)

2 Work the first dc into the second chain from the hook. Then work 1 dc into each of the remaining 2 chains. This creates a 3-dc increase at the beginning of the row.

3 Continue the row in the usual way, working 1 dc into each dc in the row below. Any number of stitches can be added in this way and the same technique can be used for taller stitches.

Step increase at end of row

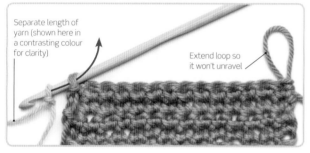

Separate length of
yarn (shown here in
a contrasting colour
for clarity)

Extend loop so
it won't unravel

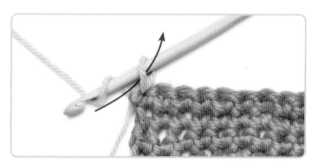

1 Before starting the row with the step increase at the end, remove the hook from the loop at the beginning of the row. Then, using a short length of matching yarn, place a slip knot on a spare hook and draw this loop through the last stitch in the row.

2 There is now one loop on the hook – this forms the first extra chain at the end of the row. Continue making chains until you have made as many as the required number of extra stitches.

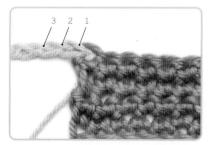

3 2 1

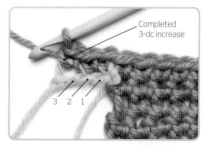

Completed
3-dc increase

3 2 1

3 So for a 3-stitch step increase, make a total of 3 chains. Then fasten off.

4 Return to the beginning of the row, slip the loop back onto the hook and tighten it, then work to the end of the row in the usual way until you reach the added chains.

5 Work 1 dc into each of the 3 added chains. This creates a 3-dc increase. Any number of stitches can be added in this way and the same technique can be used for taller stitches.

Double crochet decreases (Abbreviation = dc2tog)

Paired decreases: Decreases on garment pieces, like increases, are most frequently worked as "paired decreases" – a decrease of one stitch at the beginning of the row and another at the end.

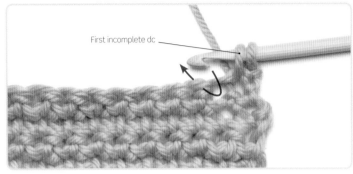

First incomplete dc

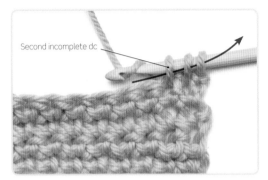

Second incomplete dc

1 To decrease one stitch at the beginning of a row of double crochet, work up to the last yrh of the first dc in the usual way, but do not complete the stitch – there are now 2 loops on the hook. Insert the hook through the next stitch as shown and draw a loop through.

2 There are now 3 loops on the hook. Wrap the yarn around the hook and draw a loop through all 3 loops at once as shown.

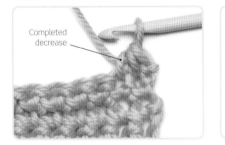

Completed decrease

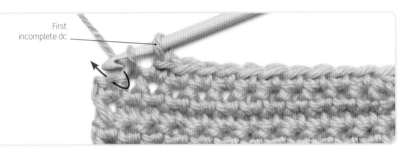

First incomplete dc

3 This completes the decrease – where there were 2 stitches, there is now only one.

4 Continue across the row, working 1 dc into each dc in the usual way up to the last 2 stitches of the row. At the end of the row, insert the hook through the top of the second to last stitch and draw a loop through – there are now 2 loops on the hook.

5 Insert the hook through the last stitch in the row below, as shown by the large arrow, and draw a loop through.

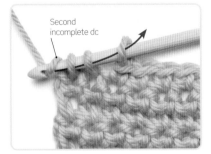

Second incomplete dc

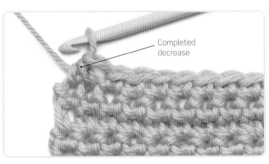

Completed decrease

6 There are now 3 loops on the hook. Wrap the yarn around the hook and draw a loop through all 3 loops at once as shown.

7 This completes the decrease at the end of the row. (The same principle can be used for a "double decrease", where 2 stitches are decreased at once. For this, work 3 incomplete dc and join them together at the top with the last yrh – this is called dc3tog.)

Treble crochet decreases (Abbreviation = tr2tog)

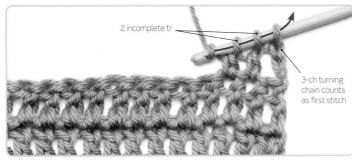

2 incomplete tr

3-ch turning
chain counts
as first stitch

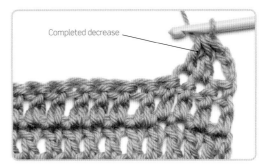

Completed decrease

1 To decrease one stitch at the beginning of a row of treble crochet, first work the turning chain. Miss the first tr and work 1 tr in each of the next 2 tr, but only up to the last yrh of each stitch. Draw a loop through all 3 loops at once as shown.

2 This completes the decrease – where there were 2 stitches, there is now only one.

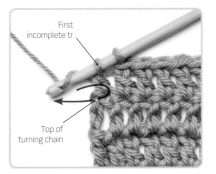

First
incomplete tr

Top of
turning chain

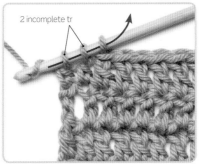

2 incomplete tr

Completed
decrease

3 Continue across the row in the usual way up to the last tr in the row below. Now work a tr into the last tr but only up to the last yrh. Wrap the yarn around the hook and insert the hook into the top of the turning chain in the row below as shown.

4 Work the tr in the top of the chain up to the last yrh of the stitch. There are now 3 loops on the hook. Wrap the yarn around the hook and draw a loop through all 3 loops at once as shown.

5 This completes the decrease at the end of the row. (The same principle can be used for a "double decrease", where 2 stitches are decreased at once. For this, work 3 incomplete tr and join them together at the top with the last yrh – this is called tr3tog.)

Step decreases

Slip stitch to
correct position

At beginning of row: Decreases, like increases, can also be worked so that they form little steps at the edge. As an example, to decrease 3 stitches at the beginning of a row of double crochet, work 1 chain and then 1 slip stitch into each of the first 4 dc. Next, work 1 chain, then work the first dc in the same place where the last slip stitch was worked. Continue along the row in the usual way.

Turn before end

At end of row: For a 3-stitch step decrease at the end of the row, simply work up to the last 3 stitches at the end of the row and turn, leaving the last 3 stitches unworked. This technique can be used for all crochet stitches.

Flat circles

Making a simple circle is a good example for how other flat motif shapes are started and then worked round and round from the centre. The circle is also used in conjunction with the crochet tube to make containers or the parts of toys, so it is well worth practising.

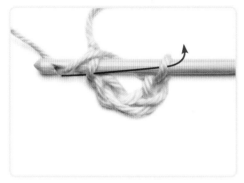

1 Follow these steps when working the simple circle for the first time. The circle is worked from the centre outwards. Start with 4 ch. Then work a slip stitch into the first chain as shown by the large arrow.

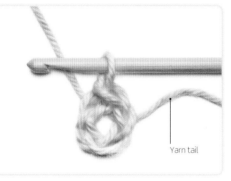

Yarn tail

2 This forms the foundation ring, which is the base for the first round of stitches.

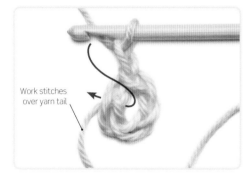

Work stitches over yarn tail

3 For a double crochet circle, start the first round with 1 chain. Then lay the yarn end around the top of the chain and start working the double crochet stitches of the first round through the centre of the ring and around the yarn tail.

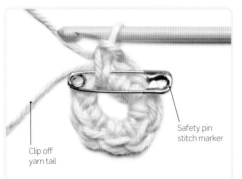

Clip off yarn tail

Safety pin stitch marker

4 When all 8 double crochet stitches of the first round are complete, mark the last stitch of the round with a stitch marker as shown. Then pull the yarn tail to close the centre hole and clip it off close to the crochet.

Move marker to last stitch at end of every round

5 Work 2 dc into each dc in the second round as explained in the pattern, working the last 2 dc into the top of the marked stitch in the last round. Then count your stitches to make sure there are 16 in total. Continue the pattern until the circle is the required size.

Tips for motifs

The principle for starting any motif shape and working it in rounds is the same as for the simple circle, and many simple crochet flowers are also worked using these techniques. If you find it awkward to fit all the stitches of the first round into a tiny foundation ring (see opposite), try the simple adjustable ring below. Two other useful tips are the techniques for starting new colours and for joining motifs together (see below).

Making a simple adjustable ring

  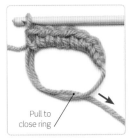

1 Making the simple adjustable ring is a quick way to start working a flat shape in the round, and it allows you to make the centre hole as tight or as open as desired. Start as if you are making a slip knot (see p.9), by forming a circle of yarn and drawing the yarn through the centre of it.

2 Leave the circle of yarn open. Then, to start a round of double crochet stitches, make 1 chain.

3 Work the first round of double crochet stitches, working them into the ring and over the yarn tail as shown by the large arrow.

4 When all the required stitches are worked into the ring, pull the yarn tail gently to close the ring. Then continue as explained in the pattern instructions.

Pull to close ring

Joining on a new colour

When starting a new colour at the beginning of a motif round, you can either change to the new colour with the last yrh of the previous round, or fasten off the old colour and join on a new colour with a slip stitch.

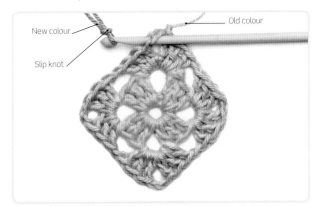

New colour

Old colour

Slip knot

1 Joining on the new colour with a slip stitch makes a firm attachment. Make a slip knot with the new colour and remove it from the hook. Then insert the hook at the specified position and draw the slip knot through.

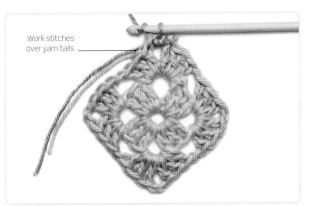

Work stitches over yarn tails

2 Start the new round with the specified number of chains, drawing the first chain through the slip knot. Work the stitches of the round over both yarn tails (the new colour and the old colour), so that there aren't many ends to darn in later. Alternatively, to reduce bulk, start the new colour in a different place and weave in one tail at a time.

Following a crochet pattern

Followed step by step and slowly, crochet patterns are not as difficult to understand as they appear. The guides here, for a simple accessory and a garment, give many tips for how to approach your first crochet patterns. This section also includes other techniques needed for working from a crochet pattern – finishings such as edgings and button loops, blocking and seams, and darning in yarn.

Simple accessory patterns

A beginner should choose an easy accessory pattern for a first crochet project. A striped cushion cover is given here as an example. Follow the numbered tips of the guide to familiarize yourself with the parts of a simple pattern.

1 The skill level required for the crochet is given at the beginning of most patterns. When starting out, work several easy patterns before progressing to the intermediate level.

2 Check the size of the finished item. If it is a simple square like this cushion, you can easily adjust the size by adding or subtracting stitches and rows.

3 It is sometimes advisable to use the yarn specified. But if you are unable to obtain this yarn, choose a substitute yarn.

8 Make a tension swatch before starting to crochet and change the hook size if necessary (see opposite).

9 Instructions for working a piece of crocheted fabric always start with how many chains to make for the foundation chain and which yarn or hook size to use. If there is only one hook size and one yarn, these may be absent here.

10 Consult the abbreviations list with your pattern for the meanings of abbreviations (see p.39).

14 The back of a cushion cover is sometimes exactly the same as the front or it may have a fabric back. In this example, the stripes are reversed on the back for a more versatile cover.

15 After all the crocheted pieces are completed, follow the Finishing (or Making Up) section of the pattern.

Striped cushion cover

Skill level
Easy

Size of finished cushion
40.5 x 40.5cm (16 x 16in)

Materials
7 x 25g/⅞oz (110m/120yds) balls of branded Scottish Tweed 4-ply in Thatch 00018 **(A)** 4 x 25g/⅞oz (110m/120yds) balls of branded Scottish Tweed 4-ply in Skye 00009 **(B)** 3.5mm (US size E-4) crochet hook
Cushion pad to fit finished cover

Tension
22 sts and 24 rows to 10cm (4in) over double crochet using 3.5mm (US size E-4) hook or size necessary to achieve correct tension. To save time, check tension.

Front
With 3.5mm (US size E-4) hook and yarn A, make 89 ch.
Row 1 1 dc in second ch from hook, 1 dc in each of rem ch, turn. (88sts)
Row 2 1 ch (does NOT count as a st), 1 dc in each dc to end, turn.
Rep row 2 throughout to form dc fabric.
Always changing to new colour with last yrh of last dc of previous row, work in stripes as follows: 26 rows more in A, 8 rows B, (8 rows A, 8 rows B) twice, 28 rows A.
Fasten off.

Back
Work as for Front, but use B for A, and A for B.

Finishing
Darn in loose ends.
Block and press lightly on wrong side, following instructions on yarn label.
With WS facing, sew three sides of back and front together. Turn right-side out, insert cushion pad, and sew remaining seam.

4 Always purchase the same total amount in metres/yards of a substitute yarn; NOT the same amount in weight.

5 If desired, select different colours to suit your décor; the colours specified are just suggestions.

6 Alter the hook size if you cannot achieve the correct tension with the specified size (see 8 left).

7 Extra items needed for your project are usually listed under Materials, Notions, or Extras.

11 Work in the specified stitch pattern, for the specified number of rows or cm/in.

12 Colours for stripes are always changed at the end of the previous row before the colour change so the first turning chain of the new stripe is in the correct colour (see p.17).

13 Fastening off completes the crochet piece.

16 Make sure you look at the yarn label instructions before attempting to press any piece of crochet. The label may say that the yarn cannot be pressed or it can be pressed only with a cool iron. (See p.32 for blocking tips.)

17 See pp.32-33 for seaming options. Take time with seams on crochet, and when working your very first seams, get an experienced crocheter to help you.

Garment patterns

Garment instructions usually start with the Skill Level, followed by the Sizes, Materials, Tension, and finally the Instructions. Most important for successfully making a garment – or other fitted items such as hats, mittens, gloves, and socks – is choosing the right size and making a tension swatch.

Tips

Choose a skill level that suits your crochet experience. If in doubt or if you haven't crocheted for many years, stick to an Easy or Beginner's level until you are confident that you can go to the next level.

White is a good colour to use for your first crocheted sweater because the stitches are so easy to see clearly. But if you do choose white yarn, be sure to wash your hands every time you start crocheting; and when you stop, put away the yarn and sweater in a bag to keep it from becoming soiled.

Avoid black or other very dark yarn for a first crocheted sweater as the stitches are very difficult to distinguish, even for an accomplished crocheter.

Purchase yarn balls that have the same dye lot number.

Have a set of hook sizes at hand if you are starting to crochet sweaters. When checking tension (see below right), you may need other hook sizes in order to achieve the correct tension.

Always make the pieces in the order given in the instructions, whether you are crocheting a garment, accessory, or toy. On a garment, the back is usually crocheted first, followed by the front (or fronts, if it is a cardigan or jacket), and lastly the sleeves. Pockets that are integrated into the fronts are crocheted before the fronts and those applied as patches are worked last.

Beginners should take care when modifying patterns as sizing/shaping and stitch patterns are often worked out in detail by the pattern designer and may turn out very differently if altered. However, beginners should not be afraid to try modifying a pattern to suit their preferences, as it can always be pulled back if it does not work as planned.

Choosing a garment size

Sizing advice: Crochet garment sizes are usually listed as specific bust/chest sizes or in generic terms as Small, Medium, Large. (Children's sweater sizes are given in ages and chest sizes.) The best advice is not to stick strictly to choosing your preferred size by this criteria. Decide instead how you want the garment to fit you – how close-fitting or loose-fitting it should be. If you are planning to crochet a sweater, find one in your wardrobe that is comfortable and flattering and has a fabric weight and shape similar to the garment you are going to crochet. Smooth out the sweater and measure the width. Find the same, or closest, width to this on the sweater diagram of your crochet pattern – this is the size for you.

Make a photocopy of your pattern and circle or highlight all the figures that apply to your size throughout the pattern, starting with the number of balls of yarn to purchase, followed by the number of chains in the foundation chain for the sweater back, the length to the armhole, and so on. The figure for the smallest size is given first and all the figures for the larger sizes follow in parentheses. Where there is only one figure given in the instructions – be it a

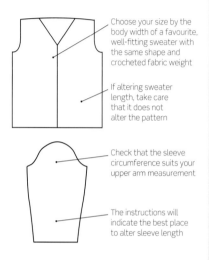

Choose your size by the body width of a favourite, well-fitting sweater with the same shape and crocheted fabric weight

If altering sweater length, take care that it does not alter the pattern

Check that the sleeve circumference suits your upper arm measurement

The instructions will indicate the best place to alter sleeve length

measurement, the number of rows, or the number of stitches – this figure applies to all sizes. Before starting your crochet, always check your tension (see below).

Measuring tension

It is essential to check your tension (stitch size) before beginning a crochet pattern if the final size of the piece matters. Not everyone crochets stitches with exactly the same tightness or looseness, so you may well need to use a different hook size to achieve the stitch size required by your pattern.

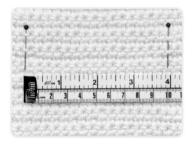

1 Using the specified hook, crochet a swatch about 13cm (5in) square. Mark 10cm (4in) across the centre with pins and count the number of stitches between the pins.

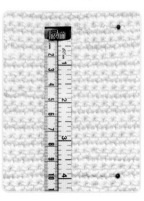

2 Count the number of rows to 10cm (4in) in the same way. If you have fewer stitches and rows than you should, try again with a smaller hook size; if you have more, change to a larger hook size. Use the hook size that best matches the correct tension. (Matching the stitch width is much more important than matching the row height.)

Basic stitches in symbols and abbreviations

Crochet row instructions can be written out with abbreviations or using symbols for the stitches. There is a more detailed explanation for reading stitch pattern instructions on page 38, but directions for the basic stitches are given in this section in both symbols and abbreviations. This provides an introduction to crochet instructions and a quick reference for how to work crochet fabrics with basic stitches. Please note that left-handed crocheters will need to work the diagram backwards. (There are basic instructions for left-handed crocheters on how to hold the hook and yarn on page 8.)

Stitch heights

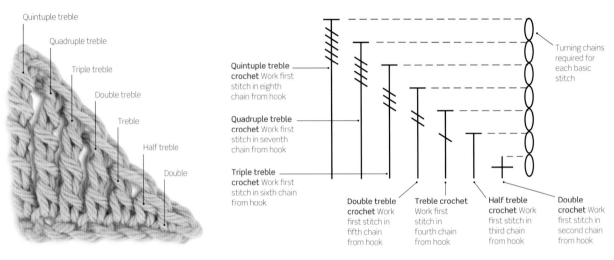

Quintuple treble

Quadruple treble

Triple treble

Double treble

Treble

Half treble

Double

Quintuple treble crochet Work first stitch in eighth chain from hook

Quadruple treble crochet Work first stitch in seventh chain from hook

Triple treble crochet Work first stitch in sixth chain from hook

Turning chains required for each basic stitch

Double treble crochet Work first stitch in fifth chain from hook

Treble crochet Work first stitch in fourth chain from hook

Half treble crochet Work first stitch in third chain from hook

Double crochet Work first stitch in second chain from hook

Stitch symbols: The diagram, above right, shows all the basic stitches in symbols and illustrates approximately how tall the stitches are when standing side by side. A double crochet is roughly one chain tall, a half treble crochet two chains tall, a treble crochet three chains tall, and so on. (The picture, above left, shows what each stitch actually looks like.) These heights determine the number of turning chains you need to work at the beginning of each row for each of the basic stitches. The diagonal bars are useful as they indicate how many times you need to wrap the yarn around the hook before working the stitch. Also provided here is a reference for which chain to work into when working the first stitch into the foundation chain.

Double crochet instructions

Double symbol: Crochet symbol instructions, especially for the basic stitches, are very easy to understand. Roughly imitating the size and shape of the stitch, the symbols are read from the bottom of the diagram upwards. To get used to very simple crochet instructions, try working double crochet following the written directions and the symbol diagram at the same time (see p.39 for abbreviations list), then try this with the other basic stitches as well.

Double crochet in abbreviations
Make any number of ch.
Row 1 1 dc in second ch from hook, 1 dc in each of rem ch to end, turn.
Row 2 1 ch (does NOT count as a st), 1 dc in each dc to end, turn.
Rep row 2 to form dc fabric.

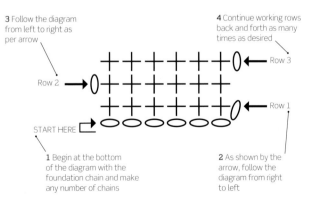

3 Follow the diagram from left to right as per arrow

4 Continue working rows back and forth as many times as desired

Row 3

Row 2

Row 1

START HERE

1 Begin at the bottom of the diagram with the foundation chain and make any number of chains

2 As shown by the arrow, follow the diagram from right to left

Half treble crochet instructions

Half treble symbol: The symbol for half treble is a vertical line with a horizontal bar at the top, and it is about twice as tall as the double crochet symbol, just like the stitch is in reality. Read the written instructions for this basic stitch (below) and look at the chart at the same time. The direction of each arrow indicates whether to read the chart from left to right or right to left.

Half treble crochet in abbreviations
Make any number of ch.
Row 1 1 htr in third ch from hook, 1 htr in each of rem ch to end, turn.
Row 2 2 ch (counts as first st), miss first htr in row below, *1 htr in next htr; rep from * to end, then work 1 htr in top of 2 ch at end, turn.
Rep row 2 to form htr fabric.

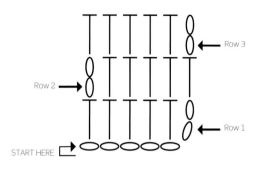

Treble crochet instructions

Treble symbol: The treble symbol has a short diagonal line across its "waist". The diagram shows clearly how the 3-ch turning chain counts as the first stitch of each row.

Treble crochet in abbreviations
Make any number of ch.
Row 1 1 tr in fourth ch from hook, 1 tr in each of rem ch to end, turn.
Row 2 3 ch (counts as first tr), miss first tr in row below, *1 tr in next tr; rep from * to end, then work 1 tr in top of 3 ch at end, turn.
Rep row 2 to form tr fabric.

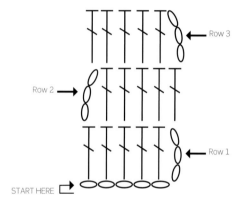

Double treble crochet instructions

Double treble symbol: Two short diagonal lines cross the "waist" of the double treble symbol, echoing the two diagonal yarn strands on the stitch itself.

Double treble crochet in abbreviations
Make any number of ch.
Row 1 1 dtr in fifth ch from hook, 1 dtr in each of rem ch to end, turn.
Row 2 4 ch (counts as first dtr), miss first dtr in row below, *1 dtr in next dtr; rep from * to end, then work 1 dtr in top of 4 ch at end, turn.
Rep row 2 to form dtr fabric.

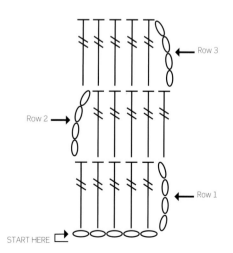

Blocking and seams

Always sew the seams on a garment or accessory using a blunt-ended needle and a matching yarn (a contrasting yarn is used here just to show the seam techniques more clearly); work them in the order given in the crochet pattern.

But before sewing any seams, block your crochet pieces carefully. Press the finished seams very lightly with a cool iron on the wrong side after completion.

Wet blocking

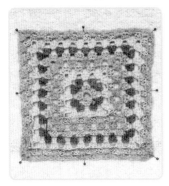

Using water: If your yarn will allow it, wet blocking is the best way to even out crochet. Wet the pieces in a sink full of lukewarm water. Then squeeze out the water and roll the crochet in a towel to remove excess dampness. Smooth the crochet into shape right-side down on layers of dry towels covered with a sheet, pinning at intervals. Add as many pins as is necessary to refine the shape. Do not move the crochet until it is completely dry.

Steam blocking

Using steam: For a speedier process, you may prefer steam blocking (if your yarn label allows it). First, pin the crochet right-side down into the correct shape. Then steam the crochet gently using a clean damp cloth, but barely touching the cloth with the iron. Never rest the weight of an iron on your crochet or it will flatten the texture. Leave the steamed piece to dry completely before unpinning it.

Backstitch seam

Backstitch produces durable seams and is frequently recommended in crochet patterns for garments, accessories, and toys.

1 Align the crochet pieces with right sides together and secure the yarn with two or three overcast stitches in the same place. Then, inserting the needle close to the edge, work the seam taking one stitch forwards and one stitch back.

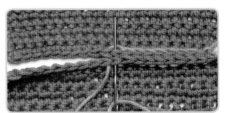

2 On the backwards stitch, be sure to insert the needle through the same place as the end of the last stitch. At the end of the seam, secure the yarn in the same way as at the beginning of the seam.

Overcast stitch seam (also called whip stitch)

Wrong side of crochet

Simple overcast seam: Align the crochet pieces with right sides together and secure the yarn as for backstitch. Then, inserting the needle close to the edge, make stitches through the two layers as shown.

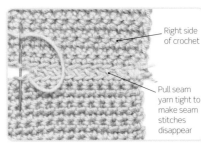

Right side of crochet

Pull seam yarn tight to make seam stitches disappear

Flat overcast seam: For a flat seam along the tops of stitches, lay the pieces right-side up and edge-to-edge. Work as for the simple overcast seam, but insert the needle through only the back loops of the stitches.

Edge-to-edge seam (also called mattress stitch)

This method creates a neat, flat seam line. It can be used, as here,
on treble crochet as well as on all other types of crochet fabrics.

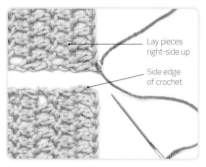

Lay pieces right-side up

Side edge of crochet

1 Align the pieces of crochet right-side up and edge-to-edge. Insert the needle through the corner of the top piece, leaving a long loose end.

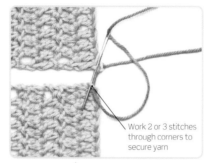

Work 2 or 3 stitches through corners to secure yarn

2 Insert the needle through the corner of the other piece, then through both pieces again in the same place at the corner to secure firmly.

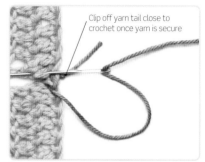

Clip off yarn tail close to crochet once yarn is secure

3 Make the next stitch along the centre of the stitch (a treble or a turning chain) at the edge on the top piece of crochet. Make the next stitch along the centre of the stitch or turning chain on the opposite edge.

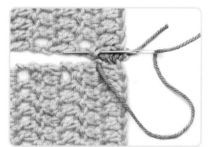

4 Make the next pair of stitches in the same way, working a stitch along one stitch or turning chain on the top piece, then, on the opposite piece.

5 Continue along the seam, taking a stitch in each side alternately. Take shorter stitches on each piece if the yarn used for the pieces is bulky.

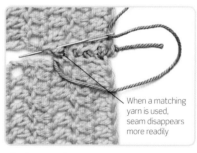

When a matching yarn is used, seam disappears more readily

6 After every few stitches, pull the yarn tight so that the seam yarn disappears and is not visible on the right side of the crochet.

Slip stitch seam

Start with a slip knot on the hook

Seam yarn

1 Instead of using a yarn needle to join the seam, you can use a crochet hook to work a quicker seam. Although seams can be worked with double crochet, slip stitch seams are less bulky. Start by placing a slip knot on the hook.

2 Align the two layers with the right sides together. Then, with the slip knot on the hook, insert the hook through the two layers at the starting end of the seam, wrap the yarn around the hook, and draw a loop through the layers and the loop on the hook.

3 Continue in this way and fasten off at the end. When working the seam along the tops of stitches, insert the hook through the back loops of the stitches only. Along row-end edges, work through the layers one stitch in from the edge.

Stitch techniques

The basic crochet stitches can be combined in various ways to create endless textures and sculptured effects. Not all the vast range of crochet stitch techniques can be included, but the most commonly used are explained here in detail. When attempting the stitch patterns on pages 40–41, refer back to these step-by-step instructions to see more clearly how to achieve the textures.

Simple textures

The simplest and most subtle crochet textures are created by working into various parts of the stitches or between the stitches in the row below. Before trying out any of these techniques, learn about the parts of the stitches so you can identify them easily.

Parts of stitches

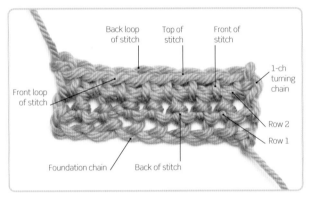

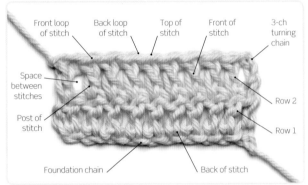

Double crochet stitches: Work two rows of double crochet (see pp.14-15) and fasten off. Look closely at your sample and make sure you can identify all the parts of the stitch labelled above. If your crochet pattern tells you to work into the stitch below, always insert the hook under BOTH loops (the front loop and the back loop) at the top of the stitch as explained on page 15 for double crochet, unless it tells you to do otherwise.

Treble crochet stitches: Work two rows of treble crochet (see pp.18–19) and fasten off. Again, make sure you can identify all the parts of the stitch labelled above. As for double crochet and all other crochet stitches, if your crochet pattern tells you to work into the stitch below, always insert the hook under both loops at the top of the stitch, unless it tells you to do otherwise.

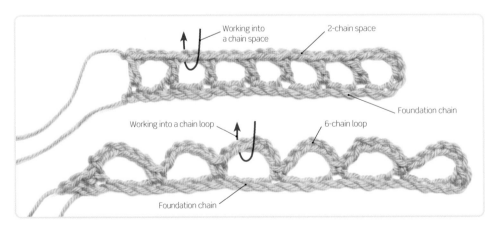

Chain spaces and chain loops: In many stitch patterns, chain stitches are introduced between basic stitches to create holes or spaces in the fabric. Spaces formed by short chains are called chain spaces, and those formed by long chains are called chain loops. When a crochet pattern instructs you to work into a chain space (or loop), always insert your hook from front to back through the space and not into the actual chain stitches.

Working into the back loop of a double crochet

Ridge effect: Working into only the back loops of the stitches in every row of double crochet creates a deep, ridged effect. The ridges are formed by the unworked loops.

Working into the front loop of a double crochet

Smooth effect: Working into only the front loop of each double crochet in the row below, on every row, creates a less pronounced texture than working into only the back loop.

Working into the back loop of a treble crochet

Treble ridge: The same techniques shown for working into the back or front of a double crochet can be used on all crochet stitches to create ridges. The fabric looks the same on both sides.

Working into spaces between stitches

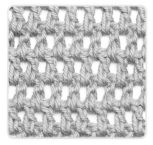

Treble space: Another way to achieve a subtly different texture with basic stitches is to work the stitches into the spaces between the stitches in the row below, instead of into the tops of the stitches.

Working into a chain space

Simple texture: Tweed stitch illustrates the simplest of all textures created by working into a chain space. Here, double crochet stitches are worked in the 1-chain spaces between the stitches in the row below, instead of into the tops of the stitches.

Tweed stitch pattern

Because it is such a popular stitch and a perfect alternative to basic double crochet, the pattern for it is given here. (See p.39 for abbreviations.) Start with an even number of chains.

Row 1 1 dc in second ch from hook, *1 ch, miss next ch, 1 dc in next ch; rep from * to end, turn.

Row 2 1 ch (does NOT count as a stitch), 1 dc in first dc, 1 dc in next 1-ch sp, *1 ch, 1 dc in next 1-ch sp; rep from * to last dc, 1 dc in last dc, turn.

Row 3 1 ch (does NOT count as a stitch), 1 dc in first dc, *1 ch, 1 dc in next 1-ch sp; rep from * to last 2 dc, 1 ch, miss next dc, 1 dc in last dc, turn.

Rep rows 2 and 3 to form patt.

Sculptural textures

These easy raised and grouped crochet stitch techniques produce attractive sculptural textures. Although they can be used to create fairly dense stitch patterns (see pp.40-41), they are also found in lace stitches (see pp.50-51).

Front post treble

Working around the post is used to make a fabric that imitates knitted ribbing, but it can also be used on its own in rows to create a ridged effect.

1 Start with a row of trebles. On following rows, work 2 chains, yrh, and insert the hook from the front around the post of the second treble.

2-ch turning chain

2 To complete the treble, yrh and draw a loop through, then (yrh and draw through the first 2 loops on the hook) twice as shown by the two large arrows.

3 Work a treble around each of the following trebles in the row below in the same way. At the end of the row, work a treble into the top of the turning chain. Repeat the second row to form a ridged texture.

Back post treble

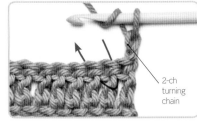

1 Start by working a base row of treble crochet. To start the second row, work 2 chains, yrh, and insert the hook from the back around the post of the second treble.

2-ch turning chain

2 To complete the treble, yrh and draw a loop through, then (yrh and draw through the first 2 loops on the hook) twice as shown by the two large arrows.

3 Work a treble around each of the trebles in the row below in the same way. Continue as for step 3 of Front post treble (above).

Shells

4 tr in same chain

4-tr shell: Shells are the most frequently used of all crochet stitch techniques. Usually made with trebles, they are formed by working several stitches into the same stitch or space. Here 4 trebles have been worked into the same chain to form a 4-tr shell.

5 tr in same chain

5-tr shell: Here 5 trebles have been worked into the same chain to form a 5-tr shell. Any number of trebles can be used to form a shell, but the most commonly used crochet shells have 2, 3, 4, 5, or 6 stitches. Shells can also be made with half trebles and taller basic stitches.

Bobbles

Joining effect: Bobbles are formed using the shell technique and the cluster technique so that the stitches are joined together at the top and the bottom.

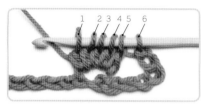

1 To work a 5-tr bobble, work 5 incomplete trebles (as for a cluster) into the same stitch (as for a shell). There are now 6 loops on the hook.

2 Wrap the yarn around the hook and draw a loop through all 6 loops on the hook.

3 This completes all of the trebles at the same time and joins them at the top. Some bobbles are completed with an extra chain as shown by the large arrow. Bobbles are usually made with 3, 4, or 5 trebles. Bobbles made with half trebles are called puff stitches.

Clusters

Crocheted clusters look like upside down shells. They are made by joining the tops of several stitches (each worked into a different stitch below) into a single top.

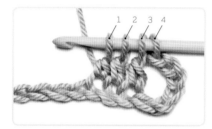

1 To make a 3-tr cluster, work a treble up to the last yrh that completes the treble. Then work an incomplete treble into each of the next 2 stitches in the same way. There are now 4 loops on the hook.

2 Wrap the yarn around the hook and draw a loop through all 4 loops on the hook.

3 This completes all of the trebles at the same time and joins them at the top. Clusters can be made with 2, 3, 4, 5, 6, or more trebles, and with half trebles or taller basic stitches as well.

Popcorns

1 Popcorns are started like shells. To make a 5-tr popcorn, begin by working 5 trebles in the same stitch.

2 Remove the hook from the loop and insert it from back to front through the top of the first treble of the group. Draw the working loop through the top of the first treble as shown by the large arrow.

3 This pulls the tops of the shells together to form a bobble-type shape. Unlike the top of a bobble, the top of a popcorn protrudes forwards because of the method of construction. Popcorns are usually made with 3, 4, or 5 trebles.

Following simple stitch patterns

Working a project from a crochet pattern for the first time can seem difficult for a beginner, especially if an experienced crocheter is not at hand as a guide. The best way to prepare for a crochet pattern is to first practise crocheting rectangles of various stitch patterns using simple stitch techniques. This is a good introduction to following abbreviated written row instructions and symbol diagrams.

Understanding written instructions

As long as you know how to work all the basic stitches and can work them from the simple patterns on pages 30-31 and have reviewed pages 34-35 where special stitch techniques are explained, there is nothing stopping you from trying to work the simple textures stitch patterns on pages 40-41 Simply consult the list on the opposite page for the meanings of the various abbreviations and follow the written row instructions one step at a time.

Begin by making the required number of chains for the foundation chain, using your chosen yarn and one of the hook sizes recommended for this yarn weight. Crochet a swatch that repeats the pattern only a few times to test it out.

(If you decide to make a blanket or cushion cover with the stitch later, you can adjust the hook size before starting it to obtain the exact flexibility of fabric you desire for your project.)

Work each row of the stitch pattern slowly and mark the right side of the fabric (if there is one) as soon as you start, by tying a contrasting coloured thread to it. Another good tip is to tick off the rows as you complete them or put a sticky note under them, so you don't lose your place in the pattern. If you do get lost in all the stitches, you can pull out all the rows and start the pattern from the foundation chain again.

Understanding stitch symbol diagrams

Crochet stitch patterns can also be given in symbols (see opposite). These diagrams are usually even easier to follow than directions with abbreviations because they create a visual reference of approximately how the finished stitch will look. Each basic stitch on the chart is represented by a symbol that resembles it in some way. The position of the base of each stitch symbol indicates which stitch or chain space it is worked into in the row below. If the symbols are joined at the base, this means that they are worked into the same stitch in the row below.

The beginning of the foundation chain will be marked as your starting point on the diagram. Read each row on the diagram either from right to left or left to right following the direction of the arrow. Although you can consult the written instructions for how many chains to make for a foundation chain and how to

repeat the stitch repeat across a row (or a row repeat up the fabric), it is easy to work these out yourself from the diagram once you become proficient in reading diagrams. But to begin with, work from the written instructions and use the diagram as a visual aid. Once you have completed the first few rows of the pattern, you can dispense with the written instructions altogether and continue with the diagram as your sole guide. If the stitch is an easy one, you will very quickly be able to work it without looking at any instructions at all.

This symbol diagram for the open shell stitch is a good introduction to working from a symbol diagram. Start at the bottom of the diagram and follow it row by row with the aid of the numbered tips.

Sample stitch pattern

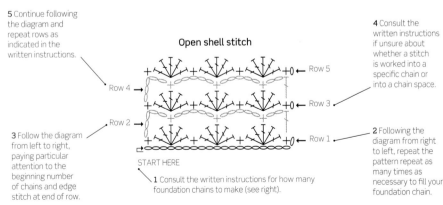

5 Continue following the diagram and repeat rows as indicated in the written instructions.

Row 4 →

3 Follow the diagram from left to right, paying particular attention to the beginning number of chains and edge stitch at end of row.

Open shell stitch

Row 2 →

START HERE

1 Consult the written instructions for how many foundation chains to make (see right).

Row 5
Row 3
Row 1

4 Consult the written instructions if unsure about whether a stitch is worked into a specific chain or into a chain space.

2 Following the diagram from right to left, repeat the pattern repeat as many times as necessary to fill your foundation chain.

Crochet instructions
Make a multiple of 6 ch, plus 2 extra.
Row 1 (RS) 1 dc in second ch from hook, *miss next 2 ch, 5 tr in next ch, miss next 2 ch, 1 dc in next ch; rep from * to end, turn.
Row 2 5 ch (counts as first tr and a 2-ch sp), 1 dc in centre tr of first shell, *5 ch, 1 dc in centre tr of next shell; rep from *, ending with 2 ch, 1 tr in last dc, turn.
Row 3 1 ch (does NOT count as a st), 1 dc in first tr, *5 tr in next dc, 1 dc in next 5-ch loop; rep from * working last dc of last rep in third ch from last dc, turn.
Rep rows 2 and 3 to form patt.

Crochet abbreviations

These are the abbreviations most commonly used in crochet patterns. The abbreviations for the basic stitches are listed first and the other abbreviations found in crochet patterns follow. Any special abbreviations in a crochet pattern will always be explained in the pattern.

Abbreviations for basic stitches

Note: The names for the basic crochet stitches differ in the UK and the US. This book uses UK crochet terminology, so if you have learned to crochet in the US, be sure to take note of the difference in terminology.

ch	chain	**foll**	follow(s)(ing)	**RS**	right side
ss	slip stitch	**g**	gram(s)	**sp**	space(s)
dc	double crochet (US single crochet – sc)	**htr2tog**	(Yrh and insert hook in next st,	**st(s)**	stitch(es)
htr	half treble (US half double crochet – hdc)		yrh and draw a loop through)	**TBL**	through back loop
tr	treble (US double crochet – dc)		twice, yrh and draw through all 5	**TFL**	through front loop
dtr	double treble (US treble crochet – tr)		loops on hook – 1 st decreased.	**tog**	together
trtr	triple treble (US double treble crochet – dtr)		(US hdc2tog)	**tr2tog**	see p.24
qtr	quadruple treble (US triple treble crochet – trtr)	**htr3tog**	(Yrh and insert hook in next st,	**tr3tog**	see p.24
quintr	quintuple treble (US quadruple treble – quadtr)		yrh and draw a loop through) 3	**WS**	wrong side
			times, yrh and draw through all 7	**yds**	yard(s)
			loops on hook – 2 sts decreased.	**yrh**	yarn round hook (US yarn over hook – yo)
Other abbreviations			(US hdc3tog)	*****	repeat instructions after asterisk
alt	alternate				or between asterisks as many times
beg	begin(ning)	**in**	inch(es)		as instructed
cont	continu(e)(ing)	**inc**	increas(e)(ing)	**( )**	repeat instructions inside round
dc2tog	see p.24	**patt(s)**	pattern(s)		brackets as many times as instructed
dc3tog	see p.24	**rem**	remain(s)(ing)	**[ ]**	used for a repeat within a repeat
dec	decreas(e)(ing)	**rep**	repeat(s)(ing)		

Crochet stitch symbols

These are the symbols used in this book, but crochet symbols are not universal so always consult the key with your crochet instructions for those used in your pattern.

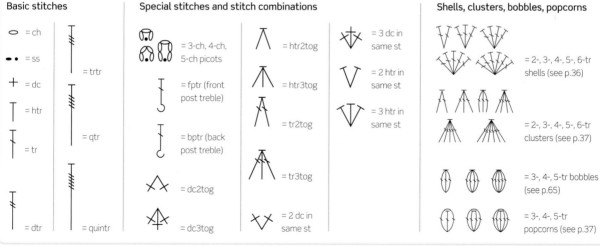

Simple textures stitch patterns

Selected for how easy they are to work, these stitch patterns cover an array of textures. Beginner crocheters should follow the written instructions for the first few rows, referring to the symbols for clarification and page 39 for simple stitch patterns. Where there is no right or wrong side marked in the instructions of a stitch (see rib stitch and close shells stitch), it looks the same on both sides and the fabric is reversible.

Crochet rib stitch

Crochet diagram

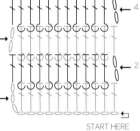

START HERE

Crochet instructions

Make a multiple of 2 ch.
Row 1 1 tr in fourth ch from hook, 1 tr in each of rem ch, turn.
Row 2 2 ch (counts as first st), miss first tr, *1 tr around post of next tr from front, 1 tr around post of next tr from back; rep from * to end, 1 tr in top of turning ch at end, turn.
Rep row 2 to form patt.

Simple crossed stitch

Crochet diagram

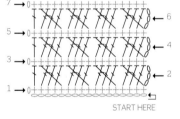

START HERE

Crochet instructions

Make a multiple of 4 ch, plus 2 extra.
Row 1 1 dc in second ch from hook, 1 dc in each of rem ch, turn.
Row 2 (RS) 3 ch (counts as first tr), miss first dc, 1 tr in each of next 3 dc, yrh and insert hook from front to back in first dc (the missed dc), yrh and draw a long loop through (extending the loop so that it reaches back to position of work and does not squash 3-tr group just made), (yrh and draw through first 2 loops on hook) twice (called long tr), *miss next dc, 1 tr in each of next 3 dc, 1 long tr in last missed dc; rep from * to last dc, 1 tr in last dc, turn.
Row 3 1 ch (does NOT count as a st), 1 dc in each tr to end (do NOT work a dc in 3-ch turning chain), turn.
Rep rows 2 and 3 to form patt.

Close shells stitch

Crochet diagram

START HERE

Crochet instructions

Make a multiple of 6 ch, plus 2 extra.
Row 1 1 dc in second ch from hook, *miss next 2 ch, 5 tr in next ch, miss next 2 ch, 1 dc in next ch; rep from * to end, turn.
Row 2 3 ch (counts as first tr), 2 tr in first dc, *miss next 2 tr, 1 dc in next tr, 5 tr in next dc (between shells); rep from *, ending last rep with 3 tr in last dc (instead of 5 tr), turn.
Row 3 1 ch (does NOT count as a st), 1 dc in first tr, *5 tr in next dc (between shells), miss next 2 tr, 1 dc in next tr; rep from *, working last dc in top of 3-ch at end, turn.
Rep rows 2 and 3 to form patt.

Cluster and shell stitch

Crochet diagram

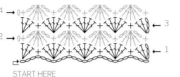

START HERE

Crochet instructions

Note: cluster (also called dc5tog) = over next 5 sts (which include 2 tr, 1 dc, 2 tr) work (yrh and insert hook in next st, yrh and draw a loop through, yrh and draw through first 2 loops on hook) 5 times (6 loops now on hook), yrh and draw through all 6 loops on hook (see p.37). Make a multiple of 6 ch, plus 4 extra.

Row 1 (RS) 2 tr in fourth ch from hook, miss next 2 ch, 1 dc in next ch, *miss next 2 ch, 5 tr in next ch, miss next 2 ch, 1 dc in next ch; rep from * to last 3 ch, miss next 2 ch, 3 tr in last ch, turn.

Row 2 1 ch (does NOT count as a st), 1 dc in first tr, *2 ch, 1 cluster over next 5 sts, 2 ch, 1 dc in next tr (centre tr of 5-tr group); rep from *, working last dc of last rep in top of 3 ch at end, turn.

Row 3 3 ch (counts as first tr), 2 tr in first dc, miss next 2 ch, 1 dc in next st (top of first cluster), *5 tr in next dc, miss next 2 ch, 1 dc in next st (top of next cluster); rep from *, ending with 3 tr in last dc, turn.

Rep rows 2 and 3 to form patt.

Simple bobble stitch

Crochet diagram

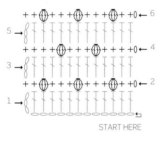

START HERE

Crochet instructions

Note: bobble = (yrh and insert hook in specified st, yrh and draw a loop through, yrh and draw through first 2 loops on hook) 4 times all in same st (5 loops now on hook), yrh and draw through all 5 loops on hook (see p.37). Make a multiple of 4 ch, plus 3 extra.

Row 1 (WS) 1 tr in fourth ch from hook, 1 tr in each of rem ch, turn.

Row 2 (RS) 1 ch (does NOT count as a st), 1 dc in each of first 2 tr, *1 bobble in next tr, 1 dc in each of next 3 tr; rep from * to last 2 tr, 1 bobble in next tr, 1 dc in next tr, 1 dc in top of 3 ch at end, turn.

Row 3 3 ch (counts as first tr), miss first dc and work 1 tr in each st to end, turn.

Row 4 1 ch (does NOT count as a st), 1 dc in each of first 4 tr, *1 bobble in next tr, 1 dc in each of next 3 tr; rep from *, ending with 1 dc in top of 3 ch at end, turn.

Row 5 Rep row 3.

Rep rows 2–5 to form patt, ending with a patt row 5.

Shells and chains

Crochet diagram

START HERE

Crochet instructions

Make a multiple of 6 ch, plus 2 extra.

Row 1 (RS) 1 dc in second ch from hook, *miss next 2 ch, work (1 tr, 1 ch, 1 tr, 1 ch, 1 tr) all in next ch, miss next 2 ch, 1 dc in next ch; rep from * to end, turn.

Row 2 4 ch (counts as 1 tr and a 1-ch sp), 1 tr in first dc, miss next tr, 1 dc in next tr (centre tr of shell), *work (1 tr, 1 ch, 1 tr, 1 ch, 1 tr) all in next dc (between shells), miss next tr, 1 dc in next tr (centre tr of shell); rep from *, ending with [1 tr, 1 ch, 1 tr] in last dc, turn.

Row 3 1 ch (does NOT count as a st), 1 dc in first tr, *work (1 tr, 1 ch, 1 tr, 1 ch, 1 tr) all in next dc, miss next tr, 1 dc in next tr (centre tr of shell); rep from *, working last dc of last rep in third of 4-ch made at beg of previous row, turn.

Rep rows 2 and 3 to form patt.

Embellishments for crochet

There are many ways to add subtle or bold embellishments to your crochet. Although it may seem unimportant, choosing the right buttons when they are required comes top of the list, so always select buttons carefully and take your finished crochet along to try them out before purchasing any. Other adornments that will dress up your crochet include beads, ribbons, pompoms and fringe, edgings, and embroidery.

Beaded crochet

Beads can be sewn onto your finished crochet if you are only adding a few. But for an all-over effect, work the beads into the fabric as you crochet. The most common beaded crochet technique uses double crochet as the background to the beads.

Working beaded double crochet

Beaded crochet is suitable for a range of simple, spaced-out, all-over geometric patterns. But beware of using too many beads on the crochet or beads that are too big, as they can add so much extra weight to the fabric that they stretch it out.

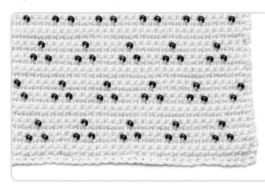

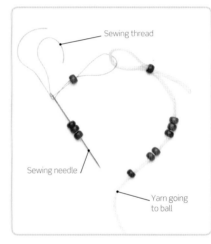

Sewing thread

Sewing needle

Yarn going to ball

1 Beaded double crochet is usually worked from a chart that shows the positions of the beads on the fabric. The chart is read as for a chart for colourwork (see p.52), and the key provided with the chart indicates which stitches are worked as plain double crochet and which have beads. Loop the end of the yarn into a loop of sewing thread as shown, then thread the beads onto the needle and down onto the yarn.

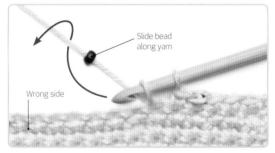

Slide bead along yarn

Wrong side

2 Follow the chart for the bead pattern, sliding the beads along the yarn until they are needed. The beads are always positioned on wrong-side rows. When a bead position is reached, work the next double crochet up to the last yrh – there are now 2 loops on the hook. Slide a bead up close to the crochet and wrap the yarn around the hook.

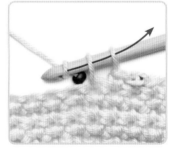

3 Draw a loop through both loops on the hook to complete the double crochet.

4 Complete the double crochet tightly, so that the bead sits snugly against the fabric on the right side of the crochet.

Embroidery on crochet

Because double crochet creates such a firm fabric, it is easy to work embroidery onto it. Many embroidery stitches are suitable for crochet and a few of the most popular ones are given here. Use the same yarn for the embroidery as the yarn used for the crochet, or a slightly thicker yarn, so that the stitches will show up well. Always work the stitches with the same type of blunt-ended yarn needle that is used for seams.

Blanket stitch

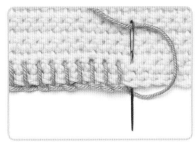

Edging: Blanket stitch creates an excellent crisp, decorative finish. Secure the yarn with 2 or 3 overcast stitches worked at the edge of the crochet. Then make evenly spaced stitches from left to right, as shown here.

Chain stitch

Motif: Chain stitch is perfect for curved motifs. Hold the yarn on the wrong side of the fabric and draw loops through with the hook. To fasten off, pull the yarn end through the last loop and then back to the wrong side over the loop. Darn in the ends on the wrong side.

Cross stitch

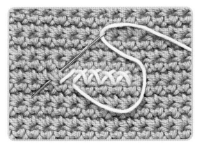

1 Work each individual cross stitch on double crochet over a single double crochet stitch. Complete each cross stitch before moving on to the next. Keep the stitches fairly loose so they don't distort the crochet.

2 Adding lines of cross stitches is an effective way to create an interesting plaid pattern on a base of plain double crochet. This is the perfect technique for dressing up a simple piece of double crochet.

Edgings on crochet

Several styles of edging patterns are provided on p.45 because they are excellent, simple adornment for your crochet. Some edgings can be worked directly onto your crochet (see p.44), and others made separately and then sewn on, as shown below.

Adding edgings

Attach an edging: To sew an edging in place, use a yarn that matches the base crochet and a blunt-ended yarn needle. Secure the yarn at the right-hand end of the seam with 2 or 3 overcast stitches. Then work evenly spaced overcast stitches through both the base crochet and the edging, as shown.

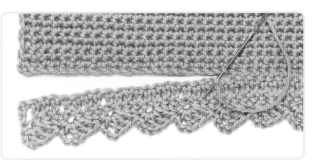

Finishing details

Finishings require slightly different crochet techniques. Some of the techniques most frequently used are shown here.
Take your time with all finishings, and practise the methods on small swatches before adding them to your completed pieces.

Double crochet edging

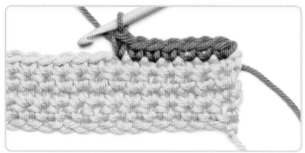

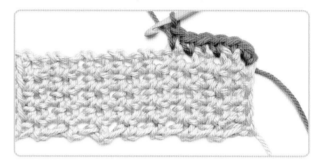

Along top or bottom of a piece of crochet: Adding a simple double crochet edging is a good way to tidy up the edges of a piece of crochet. To work a double crochet edging along the top or bottom of a piece of crochet, join the yarn to the first stitch with a slip stitch, work 1 ch, 1 dc in the same place as the slip stitch, then work 1 dc in each stitch below all along the edge.

Along row-ends of a piece of crochet: A double crochet edging is worked the same way along the row-ends of a piece of crochet, but it is not as easy to achieve an even edging. To create a perfect result, experiment with how many stitches to work per row-end. If the finished edging looks flared, try working fewer stitches per row-end; and if it looks puckered, try working more stitches per row-end.

Crocheting edging directly onto edge

Any of the edgings starting with a row of double crochet on page 45 can easily be worked directly onto the crochet.

1 Using a contrasting colour for the edging, start by working the row of double crochet onto the base, then turn and work the next row of the edging (the second row of the simple shell edging opposite is being worked here).

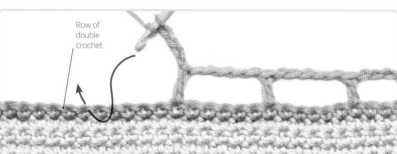

Row of double crochet

2 At the end of the second row, turn the crochet and work the remaining rows of the edging (the third and final row of the simple shell edging is being worked here).

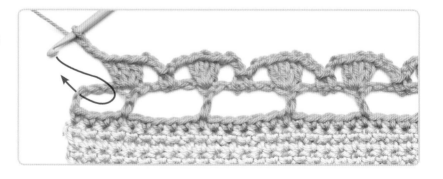

Simple edging patterns

Adding a decorative crochet edging to an otherwise mundane-looking piece of crochet can transform it from a simple project into an eye-catching piece of stitching with a touch of elegance. All the simple crochet edgings that follow are worked widthwise, so you start with a length of chain roughly equivalent to the length of edging you need. Suitable even for beginners, these edgings are perfect for dressing up towel ends, throws, baby blankets, necklines, and cuffs. When making an edging that will encircle a blanket, be sure to add extra for turning the corners; the edging can then be gathered at each corner to allow for the turning. Use a short test swatch to calculate how much extra you will need at each corner.

Picot scallop edging

Crochet instructions
Make a multiple of 4 ch, plus 2 extra.
Row 1 (WS) 1 dc in second ch from hook, *5 ch, miss next 3 ch, 1 dc in next ch; rep from * to end, turn.
Row 2 (RS) 1 ch, *work (4 dc, 3 ch, 4 dc) all in next 5-ch loop; rep from * to end. Fasten off.

Crochet diagram

Triple picot edging

Crochet instructions
Make a multiple of 6 ch, plus 2 extra.
Row 1 (WS) 1 dc in second ch from hook, 1 dc in each of rem ch, turn.
Row 2 (RS) 5 ch, work (1 dc, [5 ch, 1 dc] twice) all in first dc, *4 ch, miss next 5 dc, (1 dc, [5 ch, 1 dc] 3 times) all in next dc; rep from * to end. Fasten off.

Crochet diagram

Simple shell edging

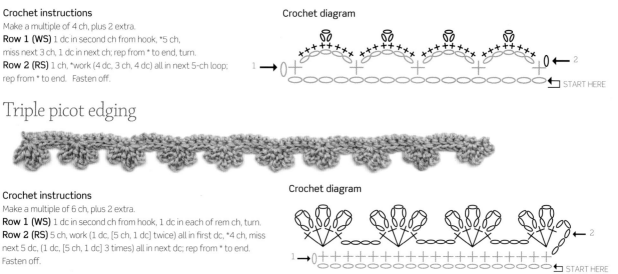

Crochet instructions
Make a multiple of 6 ch, plus 2 extra.
Row 1 (RS) 1 dc in second ch from hook, 1 dc in each of rem ch, turn.
Row 2 5 ch, miss first 3 dc, 1 tr in next dc, *5 ch, miss next 5 dc, 1 tr in next dc; rep from * to last 3 dc, 2 miss next 2 dc, 1 tr in last dc, turn.
Row 3 1 ch, 1 dc in first tr, 3 ch, 3 tr in next tr, *3 ch, 1 dc in next 5-ch space, 3 ch, 3 tr in next tr; rep from *, ending with 3 ch, miss first 2 ch of last 5 ch, 1 dc in next ch. Fasten off.

Crochet diagram

Circular crochet

Crochet can be worked not only back and forth in rows, but round and round in circles to form tubes or flat shapes started from the centre (called motifs). The basic techniques for crocheting in the round are very easy to learn, even for a beginner, so it is not surprising that many popular crochet accessories are made with circular crochet, including flowers and afghan motifs, as well as seamless toys, hats, mittens, containers, and bags.

Crocheting tubes

Tubular crochet is started on a long chain of foundation stitches that are joined at the ends to form a ring. The subsequent rounds of stitches are then worked around this foundation ring. The easiest of all crochet cylinders is a double crochet tube, shown below, which is worked in a spiral without turning chains.

Starting a tube

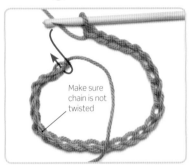

Make sure chain is not twisted

1 Start the crochet cylinder, or tube, with the length of chain specified in your crochet pattern. Then insert the hook through the first chain.

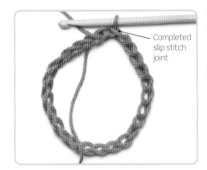

Completed slip stitch joint

2 Draw a loop through the chain and at the same time through the loop on the hook to complete the slip stitch. This joins the chain into a ring. Work the first and following rounds as directed in your pattern.

Double crochet spiral tube

First dc worked in same place as slip stitch

1 Make the foundation ring and work one chain. Work the first double crochet into the same place as the slip stitch. Then work 1 dc into each of the remaining chains of the ring.

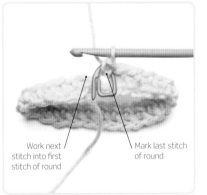

Work next stitch into first stitch of round

Mark last stitch of round

2 Place a stitch marker on the last stitch of the first round to keep track of where the rounds begin and end. To begin the second round, work the next stitch into the first stitch of the previous round.

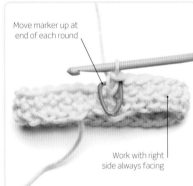

Move marker up at end of each round

Work with right side always facing

3 On the second round, work 1 dc in each dc in the round below. At the end of the round, move the stitch marker up onto the last stitch of this round. (As the spiral grows, the beginning of the round moves gradually to the right.) Continue round and round in the same way until the crochet tube is the required length.

Treble crochet tube without turns

When basic stitches taller than double crochet are used to make crochet tubes, each round is started with a turning chain.

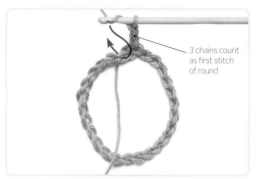

3 chains count as first stitch of round

1 To work a treble crochet tube with the right side of the work always facing (without turns), begin with 3 chains. Then work 1 tr into the next chain and each of the remaining chains around the ring.

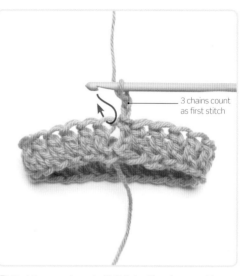

3 chains count as first stitch

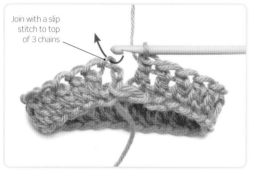

Join with a slip stitch to top of 3 chains

2 At the end of the round, join the last stitch to the top of the turning chain at the beginning of the round by working a slip stitch into the third of the 3 chains.

3 Start the second round with 3 chains. There is no need to mark the end of the round with a stitch marker as the turning chain shows where each round begins. Continue around the tube again, working 1 tr into each tr in the previous round. At the end of the second round, join the last stitch to the top of the turning chain with a slip stitch. Continue in the same way, beginning all following rounds with 3 chains.

Treble crochet tube with turns

If a treble crochet tube needs to match crochet worked in rows in other parts of an item, then the work can be turned at the end of each round.

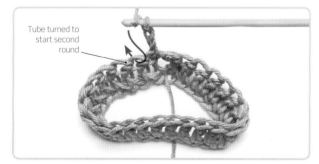

Tube turned to start second round

Second round shows backs of trebles

First round shows fronts of trebles

1 Work the first round in treble crochet as for a tube without turns. Then turn the work, make 3 chains as shown, and complete the round.

2 To begin the third round, turn the work and start with 3 chains. Continue in this way, joining the last stitch with a slip stitch to the top of the turning chain at the end of each round, then turning the work to start the next round. The fabric looks just like treble crochet that has been worked in ordinary rows.

Openwork

Whether worked with fine threads for lace collars, pillow edgings, and tablecloths or with soft wools for shawls, throws, and scarves, openwork crochet has an enduring appeal. As illustrated by the easy techniques on this page and the next, these airy lace textures are produced by working chain spaces and chain loops between the basic stitches.

Simple lace techniques

A few of the openwork stitch patterns on pages 50-51 are explained here to provide an introduction to some popular openwork crochet techniques – chain

loops, shells, and picots. Refer to the instructions for the stitches when following the steps that are shown here.

Chain loop mesh

1 After working the first row of chain loops into the foundation chain (p50), work the 5-chain loops of the following rows into the loops below, joining them on with a dc as shown here.

2 Remember to work the last dc of each row into the space inside the turning chain made at the beginning of the previous row. If you don't, your lace will become narrower.

Shell mesh stitch

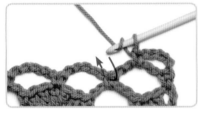

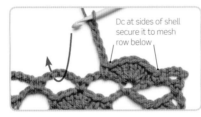

Dc at sides of shell secure it to mesh row below

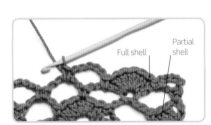

Full shell   Partial shell

1 On the shell row of this stitch (see p.50), start each shell with a dc in a chain loop. Then work all the tr of the shell into a single dc as shown.

2 Complete the shell with a dc worked into the following chain loop. Then work a chain loop and join it to the next chain loop with a dc as shown.

3 Continue alternating shells and chain loops to complete the shell row. Work mesh and shell rows alternately, working partial shells at ends on alternate shell rows.

Picot net stitch

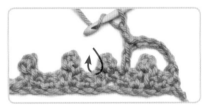

1 In this stitch pattern, work 4 chains for each picot. Close the picot-ring by working a slip stitch in the fourth chain from the hook as shown.

2 Work 3 dc between each of the picots in each picot row as shown.

3 After each picot row, work a 2-chain space above each picot and a tr between the picots as shown.

Filet crochet

Filet crochet is the easiest of all the openwork techniques. Once you learn how to work the simple structure of the open filet mesh and the solid filet blocks, all you need to do is follow a simple chart to form the motifs and the repeating patterns.

Making basic filet mesh

When working the foundation chain for the basic filet mesh, there is no need to start with an exact number of chains, just make an extra long chain and unravel the unused excess later when finishing your crochet.

Filet mesh in symbols and words: The diagram provides the best explanation of how filet mesh is worked. If in doubt, work a mesh from the written pattern as follows: Make a multiple of 3 ch (3 ch for each mesh square needed), plus 5 extra (to form the right-side edge and top of the first mesh square of the first row).
Row 1 1 tr in eighth ch from hook, *2 ch, miss next 2 ch, 1 tr in next ch; rep from * to end.
Row 2 5 ch, miss first tr, 1 tr in next tr, *2 ch, 1 tr in next tr; rep from * working last tr in third ch from last tr in row below.

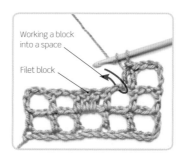

Start first space with 5 ch

Filet space

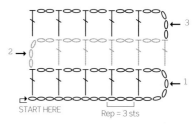

START HERE   Rep = 3 sts

Making filet blocks

The pattern motifs on filet crochet are created by filling in some of the mesh squares and leaving others empty. In other words, the designs are built up with solid squares and square holes. Having learned how to work the filet mesh, understanding how to fill them in to form blocks is easy.

Filet blocks in symbols: The diagram illustrates how the blocks are made – instead of working 2 chains to form an empty square, work 2 trebles to fill in the square. An individual block consists of a treble on each side and 2 trebles in the centre. To work a block above a filet space, work the 2 centre trebles into the 2-chain space. To work a block above another block, work a treble into each of the trebles below.

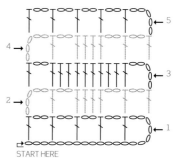

Working a block into a space

Filet block

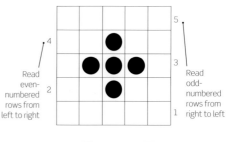

START HERE

Reading filet charts

This chart on the right shows the simple motif in the block symbol diagram above. Although actual filet charts are bigger and have elaborate patterns, the principle is the same as for this tiny chart. Each square on the chart represents either a filet space or a filet block. Please note that left-handed crocheters will need to work the diagram and instructions in a mirror image.

To start working from a chart, make 3 chains for each of the squares along the bottom row of the chart, plus 5 chains extra. (You can work the chart stitch-repeat as many times as desired.) Working the chart from the bottom upwards, make the blocks and spaces on the chart, while reading the first row and all following odd-numbered rows from right to left, and the even-numbered rows from left to right.

Read even-numbered rows from left to right

Read odd-numbered rows from right to left

Key   ☐ = filet space   ▪ = filet block

Simple openwork stitch patterns

Openwork crochet stitches are popular because of their lacy appearance, and because they are quicker to work than solid crochet textures. The written instructions below explain how many chains to start with. So if working from the diagram, consult the written instructions to make the foundation chain. When working a wide piece, such as a blanket, it is difficult to count and keep track of the number of foundation chains being made. In this case, make a chain a few centimetres longer than the correct length and unravel the excess later.

Chain loop mesh

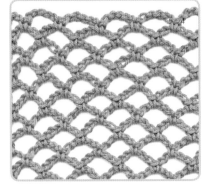

Crochet diagram

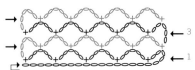

START HERE

Crochet instructions

Make a multiple of 4 ch, plus 2 extra.

Row 1 1 dc in sixth ch from hook, *5 ch, miss next 3 ch, 1 dc in next ch; rep from * to end, turn.

Row 2 *5 ch, 1 dc in next 5-ch loop; rep from * to end, turn.

Rep row 2 to form patt.

Shell mesh stitch

Crochet diagram

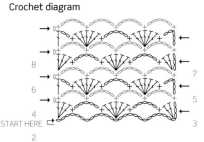

START HERE

Crochet instructions

Make a multiple of 12 ch, plus 4 extra.

Row 1 (RS) 2 tr in fourth ch from hook, *miss next 2 ch, 1 dc in next ch, 5 ch, miss next 5 ch, 1 dc in next ch, miss next 2 ch, 5 tr in next ch; rep from *, ending last rep with 3 tr (instead of 5 tr) in last ch, turn.

Row 2 1 ch (does NOT count as a st), 1 dc in first tr, *5 ch, 1 dc in next 5-ch loop, 5 ch, 1 dc in third tr of next 5-tr shell; rep from * working last dc of last rep in top of 3-ch at end, turn.

Row 3 *5 ch, 1 dc in next 5-ch loop, 5 tr in next dc, 1 dc in next 5-ch loop; rep from *, ending with 2 ch, 1 tr in last dc, turn.

Row 4 1 ch (does NOT count as a st), 1 dc in first tr, *5 ch, 1 dc in third tr of next 5-tr shell, 5 ch, 1 dc in next 5-ch loop; rep from * to end, turn.

Row 5 3 ch (counts as first tr), 2 tr in first dc, *1 dc in next 5-ch loop, 5 ch, 1 dc in next 5-ch loop, 5 tr in next dc; rep from * ending last rep with 3 tr (instead of 5 tr) in last dc, turn.

Rep rows 2–5 to form patt.

Blocks lace

Crochet diagram

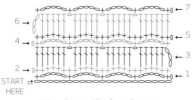

Note: When working from diagram, rep rows 2–7 to form patt.

Crochet instructions

Make a multiple of 5 ch, plus 2 extra.

Row 1 (RS) 1 dc in second ch from hook, *5 ch, miss next 4 ch, 1 dc in next ch; rep from * to end, turn.

Row 2 1 ch (does NOT count as a st), 1 dc in first dc, *5 dc in next 5-ch loop, 1 dc in next dc; rep from * to end, turn.

Row 3 3 ch (counts as first tr), miss first dc, 1 tr in each of next 5 dc, *1 ch, miss next dc, 1 tr in each of next 5 dc; rep from * to last dc, 1 tr in last dc, turn.

Row 4 1 ch (does NOT count as a st), 1 dc in first tr, *5 ch, 1 dc in next 1-ch sp; rep from * working last dc of last rep in top of 3 ch at end, turn.

Rep rows 2–4 to form patt.

Tiara lace

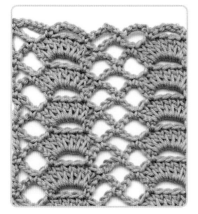

Crochet diagram

Crochet instructions

Make a multiple of 12 ch.

Row 1 (WS) 1 dc in second ch from hook, *5 ch, miss next 3 ch, 1 dc in next ch; rep from * to last 2 ch, 2 ch, miss next ch, 1 tr in last ch, turn.

Row 2 (RS) 1 ch (does NOT count as a st), 1 dc in first st, miss next 2-ch sp, 7 tr in next 5-ch loop, 1 dc in next 5-ch loop, *5 ch, 1 dc in next 5-ch loop, 7 tr in next 5-ch loop, 1 dc in next 5-ch loop; rep from *, ending with 2 ch, 1 dtr in last dc, turn.

Row 3 1 ch (does NOT count as a st), 1 dc in first dtr, 5 ch, 1 dc in second of next 7-tr shell, 5 ch, 1 dc in sixth tr of same shell, *5 ch, 1 dc in next 5-ch loop, 5 ch, 1 dc in second of next 7-tr shell, 5 ch, 1 dc in sixth tr of same shell; rep from *, ending with 2 ch, 1 dtr in last dc, turn.

Rep rows 2 and 3 to form patt.

Fans stitch

Crochet diagram

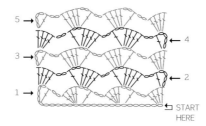

Crochet instructions

Make a multiple of 7 ch, plus 4 extra.

Row 1 1 tr in fifth ch from hook, 2 ch, miss next 5 ch, 4 tr in next ch, *2 ch, 1 tr in next ch, 2 ch, miss next 5 ch, 4 tr in next ch; rep from * to end, turn.

Row 2 4 ch, 1 tr in first tr, *2 ch, miss next 2-ch sp and work (4 tr, 2 ch, 1 tr) all in following 2-ch sp; rep from * to last 2-ch sp, miss last 2-ch sp and work 4 tr in 4-ch loop at end, turn.

Rep row 2 to form patt.

Colourwork

One-colour crochet has its charms, but using your creative imagination to combine colours is both more challenging and rewarding. All of the crochet colourwork techniques are easy to master and worth experimenting with. They include colourwork stitch patterns, stripes, jacquard, and intarsia (see p.17).

Jacquard and intarsia colourwork

Jacquard and intarsia crochet are both worked in double crochet stitches. Jacquard is usually worked with only two colours in a row; the colour not in use is carried across the top of the row below and stitches are worked over it to enclose it. When a colour is used only in an area of the crochet rather than across the entire row, the intarsia technique is required; a different length of yarn is used for each section of colour.

Colourwork charts

The charted crochet design will reveal which technique to use – jacquard or intarsia. If the pattern on the chart shows two colours repeated across each horizontal row of squares, then the jacquard technique is required. Motifs worked in isolation require the intarsia technique. Each square on the charts represent one double crochet.

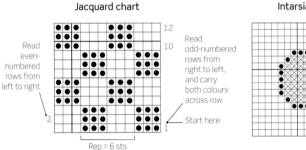

Jacquard chart

Read even-numbered rows from left to right

Read odd-numbered rows from right to left, and carry both colours across row

Start here

Rep = 6 sts

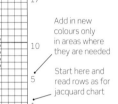

Intarsia chart

Add in new colours only in areas where they are needed

Start here and read rows as for jacquard chart

Jacquard technique

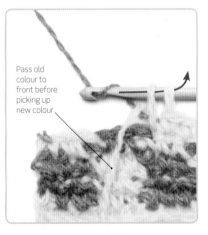

Pass old colour to front before picking up new colour

1 To change to a new colour in jacquard, work up to the last yrh of the double crochet stitch before the colour change, then pass the old colour to the front of the work over the top of the new colour and use the new colour to complete the stitch.

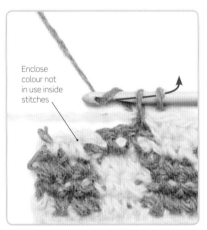

Enclose colour not in use inside stitches

2 Work the next stitch in the new colour in the usual way, but keep the old yarn positioned along the top of the row below so that the double crochet stitches in the new colour enclose it.

Intarsia technique

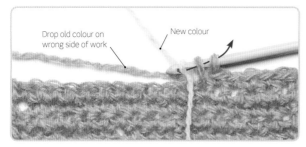

Drop old colour on wrong side of work

New colour

1 To change to a new colour in intarsia, work to the position on the chart where the motif begins, but stop before working the last yrh of the previous stitch. Then use the new colour to complete the double crochet.

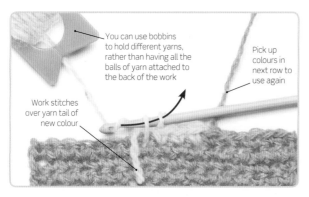

You can use bobbins to hold different yarns, rather than having all the balls of yarn attached to the back of the work

Pick up colours in next row to use again

Work stitches over yarn tail of new colour

2 Work all the required stitches in the new colour as shown. Then join on another ball (or length of yarn) for the next area of background colour. Use a separate yarn for each area of colour.

Simple colourwork stitch patterns

Crochet colourwork stitch patterns are great fun and easy to work. This selection of stitches includes an array of textures, so you are sure to find one that catches your eye. Although some of the stitches have a right and wrong side, the back and front of these fabrics still look very similar. The reversibility of crochet is one of its best features. If you want to make a scarf, shawl, baby blanket, throw, or cushion cover with one of these stitches, take your time to choose the right colour combination. See page 39 for abbreviations and basic stitch symbols. Any special symbols are given with the individual diagram.

Simple zigzag stitch

Crochet instructions
This pattern is worked in 3 colours (A, B, C). With C, make a multiple of 16 ch, plus 2 extra.

Row 1 (RS) With A, 2 dc in second ch from hook, *1 dc in each of next 7 ch, miss next ch, 1 dc in each of next 7 ch, 3 dc in next ch; rep from * to end, working 2 dc (instead of 3 dc) in last ch, turn.
Row 2 With A, 1 ch (does NOT count as a st), 2 dc in first dc, *1 dc in each of next 7 dc, miss next 2 dc, 1 dc in each of next 7 dc, 3 dc in next dc; rep from * to end, working 2 dc (instead of 3 dc) in last dc, turn.
Rows 3 and 4 With B, rep row 2.
Rows 5 and 6 With C, (rep row 2) twice.
Rows 7 and 8 With A, (rep row 2) twice.
Rep rows 3–8 to form patt.

Crochet diagram

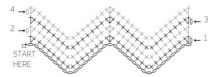

START HERE

Note: When working from diagram, rep rows 2 and 3 for stitch pattern.

Coloured cluster and shell stitch

Crochet instructions
This pattern is worked in 2 colours (A, B). Work as for cluster and shell stitch on page 41 as follows:
With A, work the foundation ch. Then work in stripe patt, repeating the following stripe sequence – 2 rows A, 2 rows B.

Spike stitch stripes

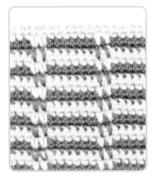

Crochet instructions

NOTE: spike st = do not work into next st, but instead insert hook front to back through top of st one row below this st, yrh and draw a loop through, lengthening the loop to the height of the row being worked (and enclosing the missed st), yrh and draw through both loops on hook to complete an elongated dc.

This pattern is worked in 2 colours (A, B).

With A, make a multiple of 8 ch, plus 1 extra.

Row 1 (RS) With A, 1 dc in second ch from hook, 1 dc in each of rem ch, turn.

Row 2 With A, 1 ch (does NOT count as a st), 1 dc in each dc to end, turn.

Row 3 With B, 1 ch (does NOT count as a st), *1 dc in each of next 3 dc, (1 spike st in top of st one row below next st) twice, 1 dc in each of next 3 dc; rep from * to end, turn.

Row 4 With B, rep row 2.

Row 5 With A, rep row 3.

Rep rows 2–5 to form patt.

Crochet diagram

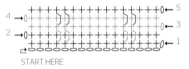

KEY

spike st in st
one row below
next st

START HERE

Bobble stripe

Crochet instructions

NOTE: bobble = [yrh and insert hook in specified st, yrh and draw a loop through, yrh and draw through first 2 loops on hook] 3 times all in same st (4 loops now on hook), yrh and draw through all 4 loops on hook to complete 3-tr bobble (see p.37).

This pattern is worked in 3 colours (A, B, C).

With A, make a multiple of 2 ch, plus 1 extra.

Work the following rows in stripes, repeating this stripe sequence – 1 row A, 1 row B, 1 row C.

Row 1 (WS) 1 htr in third ch from hook, *miss next ch, work (1 htr, 1 ch, 1 htr) all in next ch; rep from * to last 2 ch, miss next ch, 2 htr in last ch, turn.

Row 2 (RS) 3 ch (counts as first tr), 1 tr in first htr, *1 ch, 1 bobble in next 1-ch sp; rep from *, ending with 1 ch, work (yrh and insert hook in top of 2 ch at end of row, yrh and draw a loop through, yrh and draw through first 2 loops on hook) twice all in same place (3 loops now on hook), yrh and draw through all 3 loops on hook, turn.

Row 3 2 ch (counts as first htr), *work (1 htr, 1 ch, 1 htr) all in next 1-ch sp; rep from *, ending with 1 htr in top of 3 ch, turn.

Row 4 3 ch (counts as first tr), 1 bobble in next 1-ch sp, *1 ch, 1 bobble in next 1-ch sp; rep from *, ending with 1 tr in top of 2 ch at end, turn.

Row 5 2 ch (counts as first htr), 1 htr in first tr, *work (1 htr, 1 ch, 1 htr) all in next 1-ch sp; rep from *, ending with 2 htr in top of 3 ch at end, turn.

Rep rows 2–5 to form patt, while continuing stripe sequence.

Crochet diagram

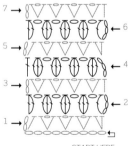

START HERE

Toys

Although crocheted toys look difficult, they are relatively easy to make, and quick as well. This step-by-step guide to crocheting a toy provides tips for making the pieces, stuffing, stitching the parts together, and for adding facial features (see pp.122-123 for the pattern).

Toy techniques

This cute teddy bear has been designed for intermediate crocheters, and its pattern on pages 122-123 has an easy-to-follow style. Because the toy has a step-by-step guide, it is an ideal first toy project. Being able to see what the pieces look like before they are stuffed will give you confidence that your crochet toy is turning out the shape it should.

The tips in the steps apply to crocheted toys in general. Start your toy project by selecting the yarns and hook required. For the sample teddy bear, you only need two colours of yarn. Select a crochet hook that will produce a tight double crochet fabric, one to two sizes smaller than the size recommended for the yarn weight category.

The extras needed for the teddy bear are the same as those for most toys – embroidery thread for the facial features, safety eyes or buttons for the eyes, and toy filling. Be VERY careful if you are making any toy for a small child; for these toys, it is best to embroider the eyes or select toy safety eyes that meet safety regulations.

Marking out the eyes
Place a stitch marker or scrap of different coloured yarn as you crochet at the position for each eye, so that when you have finished making the head, you will be able to attach the safety eyes symmetrically.

Stuffing the head
Begin stuffing the head just after you have begun decreasing, when the opening is still large enough to do so easily. Make sure you insert enough toy stuffing to fill the head completely.

Sewing up the last hole
When you have finished the head, there will be a small hole left. To sew this up, ensure you leave a long tail of yarn for sewing. Thread the yarn tail all round the opening with a yarn needle.

Start with the nose

Finishing the head
Now pull tightly on the thread to close the hole. Secure the closure with a few stitches to ensure that it does not open. You can also use this long tail to sew the body onto the head; if you wish to do so, do not fasten it off.

Adding the muzzle
Attach the safety eyes and then sew the muzzle onto the face by sewing with a whip stitch (see p.32) in the same colour as the muzzle.

Nose and mouth details
Using the embroidery thread, embroider a mouth and nose onto the muzzle as shown, or to your own design, creating an individual personality for the teddy.

Push stuffing down with crochet hook

Adding the head
Attach the head to the body using neat stitches (mattress stitch works well - see p.33), taking a stitch from the body then the head alternately as you go round, but use any neat technique you are comfortable with, ensuring that the head is on securely and does not flop over.

Stuffing limbs
To stuff the limbs, use the blunt end of the crochet hook or any long object, such as a knitting needle, to push down the toy filling. Ensure that the stuffing is pushed right down to the bottom. Use this technique to insert more stuffing and ensure that the limbs are stuffed tightly.

Adding the limbs
Attach the limbs to the body in the position shown, in a similar way to the head. While ensuring that you attach securely so that the limbs do not fall off, also make sure that they are not sewn so that they are immovable. Sew from one small spot at the side of the arm or leg, rather than at the tip, to the body to allow them to move.

Project patterns

Beaded necklace

The most basic of stitches is used to stunning effect with this necklace, which uses just chains and beads. This stylish piece of jewellery includes a series of long chains, but you can reduce the number of stitches to shorten its length.

PROJECTS
For more chain stitch patterns
>> go to page 98

Essential information

DIFFICULTY LEVEL Easy

SIZE Approx 48cm (19in) long

YARN Use any yarn for this project – it only uses a very small amount so is perfect for using up scraps. The chain will simply get thicker or thinner – just make sure that the thread can fit through the holes of the beads you have chosen

x 1

CROCHET HOOK 2mm hook
1.5mm beading hook, or size needed to fit through your beads

NOTIONS Yarn needle
Selection of beads

TENSION Exact tension is not essential

NOTE To thread the beads onto the chain, you need to ensure that the beading hook can pass through the holes in the beads, so don't choose any beads with tiny holes.

Pattern
Make a chain of the desired length to your first bead placement.
Pull up the loop on the hook to make it larger and remove the hook from the loop.
Place a bead onto the shaft of the beading hook, then insert the hook into the elongated loop.
Pull the loop through the bead and work 1 ch to secure it, pulling on the yarn to make sure that the yarn is tight around the bead.
Repeat these actions at intervals to place all the beads desired.
Work a length of chain after the last bead has been placed, and join this with a ss to the first chain made on the necklace to form a ring and complete the necklace.
Fasten off yarn, weave in ends.

1 Make around 14 even chain stitches and then slide a bead up close to the hook.

2 Thread the bead onto the yarn and make a chain stitch tightly around the bead to secure it in position on the necklace.

>> This necklace is made with DMC Petra No. 3, 100g/280m/306yds, in 53903.

Striped washcloths

These easy-to-make washcloths are constructed in double crochet, with a colourful stripe. They are an ideal practice project for beginners.

PROJECTS
For more double crochet patterns
>> go to page 62

Essential information

DIFFICULTY LEVEL Easy

SIZE 20cm (8in) square

YARN Any 4-ply non-mercerized cotton would be an acceptable alternative

A x 2   **B** x 1   **C** x 1

CROCHET HOOK 3mm hook

NOTIONS Yarn needle

TENSION 17 dc x 20 rows per 10cm (4in) square

NOTE When changing colours, always add the new colour on the last step of the last stitch of the previous row (see p.17 for instructions).

Ivory and geranium washcloth
With yarn A, work 35 ch.
ROW 1 1 dc in second ch from hook, *dc into next st, rep from * to end, turn. (34 dc)
ROW 2 1 ch, *dc into next st, rep from * to end, turn.
Continue to work in dc until piece measures 12cm (4³/₄in), changing to B on last yrh of last row.
NEXT ROW (RS) With B, 1 ch, *dc into next st, rep from * to end, turn.
NEXT ROW (WS) 1 ch, *dc into next st, rep from * to end, change to A on last yrh, turn.
Work two rows with A. Repeat stripe sequence twice more (three stripes worked in B).
Finish with two rows of dc with A.
Fasten off yarn. Weave in ends.

Edging
With yarn B and RS facing, rejoin yarn to any point along the edge of the washcloth with a ss, work a row of dc evenly around the entire edge of the washcloth, placing 3 dc into each corner stitch to turn the corners. When you are back at the first stitch, ss into first stitch to join round and fasten off yarn.
Weave in all ends.

Ivory and turquoise washcloth
Work as for first washcloth until piece measures 7cm (2³/₄in), change to C on last yrh of final dc.
Work 4 rows with C, change to A.
Work 4 rows with A, change to C.
Work 4 rows with C, change to A.
Continue working dc with A for 7cm (2³/₄in).
Fasten off yarn. Work the edging in the same way as for the first washcloth.

>> These washcloths are made with DMC Natura Cotton, 50g/155m/169yds, in A: Ivory (N02), B: Geranium (N52), and C: Turquoise (N49).

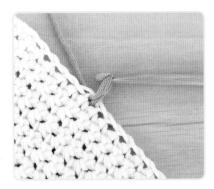

1 To make the edging, attach the new colour to the top edge of the washcloth with the right side facing, and double crochet into each stitch all the way to the corner.

2 Work 3 dc into the corner stitch to turn, and continue to double crochet all the way up the row-end edge of the washcloth, making 3 dc at each corner. Join to first stitch of edging with a slip stitch.

Making these washcloths is a great way to practise double crochet and end up with a useful item when you're finished. Don't worry too much about the tension of your square; it's fine for your washcloth to be slightly smaller or larger than the ones here.

Party bunting

Making triangles is great for practising double crochet increases. Begin with a small number of stitches, then increase at each end until you have the desired triangle shape. Bunting is a super project to utilize the resulting shapes.

PROJECTS
For more double crochet patterns
>> *go to pages 70*

Essential information

DIFFICULTY LEVEL Easy

SIZE Approx 14 x 14cm (5½ x 5½in) at the widest and longest points. Using 16 evenly spaced triangles, the bunting measures approx 3.5m (138in) long

YARN Any DK weight yarn will create the same effect, but you could use different weights to create differently sized triangles

A x 1   **B** x 1   **C** x 1   **D** x 1

CROCHET HOOK 4mm hook

NOTIONS Yarn needle

TENSION Exact tension is not essential

Triangles

Make 6 triangles in yarn A and 5 triangles each of B and C. Work 2 ch.
ROW 1 1 dc into second ch from hook.
ROW 2 1 ch, 3 dc into next dc. (3sts)
ROW 3 1 ch, dc in each dc to end.
ROW 4 1 ch, 2 dc in first dc, dc to last dc, 2 dc in last dc. (5sts)
Rep last 2 rows until you have 25 sts.
Work straight on these 25 sts for 6 rows, do not turn, but work 2 further stitches into the last dc, then work evenly in dc down the edge of the point, work 3 dc into the point of the triangle, work up other side of the point evenly in dc, join to the top row of dc with a ss. Fasten off yarn, weave in ends.

Finishing

With yarn D, work a chain of 35cm (13¾in) long, then work evenly in dc along the top of one yarn A triangle, then work 10 ch and work in dc along a yarn B triangle; now work 10 ch and then work in dc along a yarn C triangle. Continue in this way, joining the triangles in this colour pattern, and finish with a red triangle.
Work a ch of 36cm (14in) long, turn.
Miss 10 ch, dc into next ch, then into each ch to first triangle.
Work along the triangles and chains in dc to final 6 ch, work 5 ch, miss next 5 ch, then work 1 dc into last ch.
Fasten off yarn, weave in ends.

>> This bunting is made with Patons 100% Cotton DK, 100g/210m/230yds, in A: Red (2115), B: Jade (2726), C: Yellow (2740), and D: White (2691).

1 Crochet a length of chain stitches, 35cm (13¾in) long. Starting at one corner of a triangle, insert the hook through the first stitch to work the first dc.

2 Work a row of double crochet stitches along the top of the first triangle. Work 10 more chains before attaching the next triangle with dc stitches.

Using a neutral yarn, such as white, for the double crochet chain helps to emphasize the colourful triangles and makes for a neat and attractive finish.

Essential information

DIFFICULTY LEVEL Easy

SIZE Small: 4.5cm (1¾in) diameter; Medium: 5cm (2in) diameter; Large: 5.5cm (2¼in) diameter

YARN Any 4-ply yarn or crochet thread will substitute here or use different weight yarns for various sizes of flower

A x 1   **B** x 1   **C** x 1

CROCHET HOOK 3mm hook

NOTIONS Yarn needle

TENSION Exact tension is not essential

Flower garland

Flower motifs are quick and easy projects for using all of the stitches you have learned up until now. The use of all the different heights of the stitches together creates curves that are perfect for petals.

PROJECTS
For more multi-stitch patterns
>> go to page 74

Pattern

NOTE Make three of each colour in each sized flower, therefore making nine of each in total.

Big flower (make 9)
Work 5 ch, ss in first ch to form a ring.
ROUND 1 1 ch, work 16 dc into ring, join round with a ss into first ch.
ROUND 2 4 ch, (1 dtr, 2 ch) into next st, *1 dtr into next st, (1 dtr, 2 ch) into next st; rep from * to end of round, join round with a ss into top of 4 ch.
ROUND 3 1 ch, (1 htr, 2 tr, 1 dtr, 2 tr, 1 htr) all into next 2-ch sp, *1 dc in between next 2 dtr, (1 htr, 2 tr, 1 dtr, 2 tr, 1 htr) all into next 2-ch sp; rep from * to end of round, join round with a ss into first ch.
Fasten off yarn, weave in ends.

Medium flower (make 9)
Work 5 ch, ss in first ch to form a ring.
ROUND 1 1 ch, work 12 dc into ring, join round with a ss into top of 3 ch.
ROUND 2 3 ch, (1 tr, 2 ch) into next st, *1 tr into next st, (1 tr, 2 ch) into next st; rep from * to end of round, join round with a ss into top of ch 3.
ROUND 3 1 ch, (1 htr, 3 tr, 1 htr) all into next 2-ch sp, *1 dc in between next 2 tr, (1 htr, 3 tr, 1 htr) all into next 2-ch sp; rep from * to end of round, join round with a ss into first ch.
Fasten off yarn, weave in ends.

Small flower (make 9)
Work 4 ch, ss in first ch to form a ring.
ROUND 1 1 ch, work 10 dc into ring, join round with a ss into top of 3 ch.

ROUND 2 3 ch, (1 tr, 2 ch) into next st, *1 tr into next st, (1 tr, 2 ch) into next tr; rep from * to end of round, join round with a ss into top of ch 3.
ROUND 3 1 ch, (1 htr, 3 tr, 1 htr) all into next 2-ch sp, *1 dc in between next 2 tr, (1 htr, 3 tr, 1 htr) all into next 2-ch sp; rep from * to end of round, join round with a ss into first ch.
Fasten off yarn, weave in ends.

Finishing
Work a chain of desired length, threading through the middle of the flowers to create a garland. Alternatively, mount individual flowers onto a safety pin or brooch back to create a corsage.

<< This garland is made with DMC Natura Just Cotton, 50g/155m/169yds, in A: Avessac (17), B: Jade (20), and C: Eucalyptus (8).

1 Work around the central circle to create five petals. Work a double crochet into the space between the next 2 dtr after each petal.

2 Crochet a series of stitches around each flower for petals. You will need double crochet, half treble, and treble stitch. Work the same number of stitches into each chain space.

Essential information

DIFFICULTY LEVEL Easy

SIZE Large: approx 20 x 17cm (8 x 6¾in)
Medium: approx 15 x 15cm (6 x 6in)
Small: approx 14 x 10cm (5½ x 4in)

YARN Any super bulky yarn will work here. You
could even try making your own yarn from old
T-shirts and jersey fabric

A x 1   **B** x 1

CROCHET HOOK 12mm hook

NOTIONS Stitch marker
Large-eyed yarn needle

TENSION Exact tension is not essential

Structured baskets

Using such bulky yarns means these baskets work up quickly. The yarn is recycled so can vary from cone to cone. Adjust your hook as necessary for the thickness of the yarn, and crochet tightly for a rigid fabric.

PROJECTS
For more basket projects
>>*go to page 72*

For smart storage, this trio of baskets stack neatly inside each other. Easy-to-grasp handles are crocheted into the larger two baskets for carrying.

<< These baskets are made with DMC Hoooked Zpaghetti yarn, 800g/120m/131yds, in A: Beige and B: Pinky red.

NOTE These baskets are worked in spirals. Do not join rounds, but place a marker at the first stitch of the round, moving it up as each round is completed.

Large basket
With yarn A, work 2 ch and work 6 dc into second ch from hook, join round with a ss to first st.

ROUND 1 1 ch, work 2 dc in each st around, do not join round, place marker. (12sts)

ROUND 2 *2 dc in next st, 1 dc in next st, rep from * to end. (18sts)

ROUND 3 *2 dc in next st, 1 dc in next 2 sts, rep from * to end. (24sts)

ROUND 4 *2 dc in next st, 1 dc in next 3 sts, rep from * to end. (30sts)

ROUND 5 *2 dc in next st, 1 dc in next 4 sts, rep from * to end. (36sts)

ROUND 6 *2 dc in next st, 1 dc in next 5 sts, rep from * to end. Join round with a ss. (42sts)

ROUND 7 1 ch, 1 dc TBL into each st around. Join with ss.

ROUND 8 1 ch, 1 dc into each st around. Do not join round.
Work last round 5 times.

ROUND 14 3 ch, tr into bottom of same st, miss next st, *2 tr into next st, miss next st; rep from * to end of round, join to top of first ch with a ss.
Work 1 round as round 8.

ROUND 16 1 ch, 7 dc, 7 ch, miss next 7 dc, 14 dc, 7 ch, miss next 7 dc, dc to end.

ROUND 17 1 ch, (dc to 7-ch sp, 7 dc into ch sp) twice, dc to end, join round with a ss. Fasten off yarn, weave in ends.

Medium basket
With yarn A, work as for large basket to round 5. (36sts)

ROUND 6 1 ch, 1 dc TBL into each st around. Join with ss.

ROUND 7 1 ch, 1 dc into each st around. Do not join round.
Work last round 3 times, then change to yarn B and work 2 rounds.

ROUND 13 1 ch, 6 dc, 6 ch, miss next 6 dc, 12 dc, 6 ch, miss next 6 dc, dc to end.

ROUND 14 1 ch, (dc to 6 ch sp, 6 dc into ch sp) twice, dc to end, join round with a ss. Fasten off yarn, weave in ends.

Small basket
With yarn B, work as for large basket to round 4. (30sts)

ROUND 5 1 ch, 1 dc TBL into each st around. Join with ss.
Change to yarn A.

ROUND 6 1 ch, 1 dc into each st around. Do not join round.
Work last round 4 times. Join round with a ss.
Fasten off yarn, weave in ends.

Flower pin cushion

This colourful pin cushion is worked in spirals for the base, and the use of different stitches creates pretty patterns with minimal fuss.

PROJECTS

For more projects worked in the round
>> go to pages, 88 and 96

Essential information

DIFFICULTY LEVEL Easy

SIZE Approx 8cm (3in) in diameter

YARN Any small amount of crochet thread will substitute here

A x 1   B x 1   C x 1   D x 1   E x 1

CROCHET HOOK 2.5mm hook

NOTIONS Stitch marker
Yarn needle
Toy stuffing

TENSION Exact tension is not essential

NOTE Do not join rounds, but place a marker at the first stitch of the round, moving it up as each round is completed to mark the beginning of each round.
1 ch at beg of non-spiral rounds does not count as a stitch.

TOP TIP

A little patience may be required if new to crochet cotton.

Pattern

With yarn A, work 2 ch.
ROUND 1 6 dc into second ch from hook, join round with a ss.
ROUND 2 1 ch, 2 dc into each st around, join round with a ss. (12sts)
ROUND 3 1 ch, 1 dc in each st around, join round with a ss. (12sts)
ROUND 4 1 ch, 1 dc, (3 tr into next st, 1 dc) 5 times, 3 tr into last st, join round with a ss. Fasten off.
Change to yarn B, attaching to any central tr of 3-tr group.
ROUND 5 1 ch, *3 dc into tr, 1 tr into next tr, 1 dtr into dc, 1 tr into next tr; rep from * to end of round. Join round with a ss. (36sts)
ROUND 6 1 ch, 1 dc, (2 dc into next st, 5 dc) to end of round, ending with 4 dc only, join round with a ss. Fasten off. (42sts)
Change to yarn C, attaching to the first dc of a pair.
ROUND 7 1 ch, (1 dc, 1 ch, 1 dc, 1 htr, 1 tr, 3 tr into next st, 1 tr, 1 htr) around. Join round with a ss, fasten off. (54sts)
Change to yarn D, attaching yarn to central tr of any 3-tr group.
ROUND 8 1 ch, *3 dc into central tr, 1 dc, 1 htr, 1 tr, miss 1 dc, 1 dtr in ch sp, miss 1 dc, 1 tr, 1 htr, 1 dc; rep from * to end of round. (60sts)
ROUND 9 1 ch, 1 dc into each st to end of round. Work the next round TFL of every stitch.
ROUND 10 2 ss, 1 ch, *2 dc, 1 htr, 1 tr, 3 tr into next st, 1 tr, 1 htr, 2 dc, 1 ss; rep from * to end of round. Fasten off.

Change to yarn E, attaching to the back loop of any stitch from round 9.
ROUND 11 1 ch, 1 dc TBL into each st around. (60 dc TBL)
Work 6 rounds straight in regular dc, working in spirals, placing a marker at the beg of each round and moving it up as you go.
NEXT ROUND (8 dc, dc2tog) around. (54sts)
NEXT ROUND (7 dc, dc2tog) around. (45sts)
NEXT ROUND (6 dc, dc2tog) around. (36sts)
Continue in this way, decreasing 6 stitches per round by working one less dc in between decreases, until there are 6 sts left. Stuff the cushion before the hole gets too small.
Fasten off yarn, thread through remaining stitches, and pull up tight to close hole.
Weave in all ends.

To crochet in the round, you will first need to make a foundation row that is joined into a ring. Refer to page 20 for more information about working slip stitch and using slip stitches to form a foundation ring.

>> This pin cushion is made with DMC Petra Cotton Perle No. 3, 100g/280m/306yds, in A: Pink (53805), B: Blue (5799), C: Orange (53854), D: Green (5772), and E: Pale grey (53904).

Rustic pouffes

These simple pouffes are a great way to bring a touch of colour into your home. The size is simple to adjust by working more, or fewer, increase rounds.

PROJECTS

For more patterns in chunky yarns
>> go to page 66

Essential information

DIFFICULTY LEVEL Easy

SIZE Large: 40cm (15¾in) diameter
Small: 30cm (12in) diameter

YARN A super bulky cotton or stretchy jersey fabric yarn will be suitable for this project

A x 4   **B** x 5

CROCHET HOOK 8mm hook

NOTIONS Stitch marker
Large-eyed yarn needle
2 round box cushions, approx 40 x 5cm
(15¾ x 2in) and 30 x 5cm (12 x 2in);
or a low-tog duvet to fill the large pouffe

TENSION Rounds 1–3 measures approx 12cm (5in) diameter

NOTE The top of each pouffe is made first, then the sides. The base is made as a separate piece and sewn on. This allows the cushion filling to be removed for washing.

Top

With 8mm hook, work 6 ch, ss in the first ch to form a ring.
ROUND 1 6 dc into ring, do not join, continue working in a spiral using stitch marker to indicate the last st of each round (remove and replace after last dc of each round). Do not turn, continue to work in a spiral with RS facing. (6sts)
ROUND 2 2 dc in each dc. (12sts)

Stretchy jersey or cotton yarn, such as the Hooplayarn used here (a by-product of the textile industry), is growing in popularity with crocheters. Its chunkiness means that your pouffes will grow rapidly, while its texture creates a lovely knotted effect.

ROUND 3 (1 dc, 2 dc in next dc) to end. (18sts)
ROUND 4 (2 dc, 2 dc in next dc) to end. (24sts)
Continue increasing as set, working 1 more dc between each increase, making 6 increases evenly on each round until work measures 30 (40)cm/12 (15¾)in. Make a note of the stitch count as this will be needed for making the base of the pouffe.
NEXT ROUND 1 dc TBL in each dc to end.
NEXT AND SUBSEQUENT ROUNDS 1 dc in each st to end, continue to work in a spiral, without increasing until the sides measure 8 (15)cm/3 (6)in. Fasten off yarn and weave in ends. It is advised that all loose ends of yarn are sewn securely in place as, due to the nature of the yarn, they can work loose over time and may fray.

Base

Work as for top, increasing as set until stitch count matches stitch count noted for top. Fasten off yarn, weave in ends.

Finishing

Fill the pouffe with a cushion pad or duvet. Attach bottom to sides by sewing through last round of sides and last round of bottom to secure. Weave in loose ends securely. Shape gently to give a rounded appearance.

>> These pouffes are made with Hooplayarn, 500g/100m/109yds, in A: Sparkling embers and B: Warm ginger.

Fruit bowl

A very simple yet elegant bowl for storage, and perfect for holding fruit, this project is worked in the round, with one "through back loop only" round used to create the crisp rim from which the sides rise.

PROJECTS

For more storage patterns
>> go to pages 66 and 120

Essential information

DIFFICULTY LEVEL Easy

SIZE Approx 28 x 5cm (11 x 2in)

YARN Use any aran weight, preferably cotton, yarn held double or a chunky yarn held singly

A x 3   **B** x 1

CROCHET HOOK 5mm hook

NOTIONS Stitch marker
Yarn needle

TENSION Exact tension is not essential, but tension is worked tightly for rigidity

NOTE Work in spirals. Do not join rounds, but place a marker at first stitch of the round, moving it each round to mark the beginning of a round. Yarn is used as a double strand.

Pattern

With yarn A, work 2 ch and 6 dc into second ch from hook, join round with a ss to first st.
ROUND 1 1 ch, work 2 dc in each st around, do not join round, place marker. (12sts)

When crocheting into the back of one loop (written in the pattern as dc TBL) rather than working both loops of a double crochet stitch, you will create a horizontal bar across your fabric. This creates a firm rim line between the base and the sides.

ROUND 2 (2 dc in next st, 1 dc in next 1 st) around. (18sts)
ROUND 3 (2 dc in next st, 1 dc in next 2 sts) around. (24sts)
ROUND 4 (2 dc in next st, 1 dc in next 3 sts) around. (30sts)
ROUND 5 (2 dc in next st, 1 dc in next 4 sts) around. (36sts)
ROUND 6 (2 dc in next st, 1 dc in next 5 sts) around. (42sts)
Continue in this way, working one extra st between increases each round until you have worked 19 rounds and have 120 sts. If you want a larger bowl, you can continue increasing in this way until the desired size is achieved. Join round with a ss.
ROUND 20 1 ch, 1 dc TBL into each stitch around.
ROUND 21 1 ch, 1 dc into each st around. Repeat round 21 until work measures approx 3cm (1¼in) from base. Join round with a ss. Change to yarn B and work as round 21 until side measures 5cm (2in) from base. Join round with a ss.
Fasten off yarn, weave in ends.

>> This bowl is made with Sirdar Simply Recycled Aran, 50g/93m/102yds, in A: Raffia (34) and B: Lime (39).

For extra strength and rigidity, hold the yarn double.

TOP TIP

A stitch marker is essential when working in the round in dc as it allows you to keep track of the start of each round. By working the stitches accurately, you will create this lovely spiral pattern on the base of your bowl.

Chunky rug

This stylish rug is worked in rounds and makes an eye-catching addition to any room. The chunky yarn is soft and warm underfoot and works up quickly on a large crochet hook.

PROJECTS
For more chunky patterns
>> go to page 104

Essential information

DIFFICULTY LEVEL Intermediate

SIZE 90cm (35½in) diameter

YARN Any super chunky yarn, with a high synthetic content is suitable

x 6

CROCHET HOOK 12mm hook

NOTIONS Yarn needle

TENSION Rounds 1-2 measure 15cm (6in) diameter

SPECIAL ABBREVIATIONS
Treble clusters worked as follows, depending on pattern instruction:
HTRCL: half treble cluster. Insert hook into st, yrh, draw through, yrh and draw through 1 loop, insert hook into st, yrh, draw through, yrh and draw through all 3 loops on hook.
TRCL: treble cluster. Yrh, insert hook into st, yrh, draw through, yrh and draw through 2 loops, yrh, insert hook into st, yrh, draw through, yrh and draw through 2 loops, yrh and draw through remaining 3 loops on hook.

DTRCL: double treble cluster. Yrh twice, insert hook into st, yrh, draw through, yrh and draw through 2 loops twice, yrh twice, insert hook into st, yrh, draw through, yrh and draw through 2 loops twice, yrh and draw through rem 3 loops on hook.
TREBLE CLUSTER PAIR: trcl, 1 ch, trcl all in the same ch sp.

Pattern

Work 4 ch, ss into first ch to make a ring.
ROUND 1 2 ch, 1 htr into ring, 1 ch, *htrcl into ring, 1 ch, repeat from * 6 more times, ss into top of first htr to close round. (8 htrcl)
ROUND 2 Ss into next ch sp, 3 ch, 1 tr into ch sp, 2 ch, *trcl in next ch sp, 2 ch, repeat from * to end of round, ss into top of first tr to close round. (8 trcl)
ROUND 3 Ss into next ch sp, 3 ch, 1 tr into ch sp, 1 ch, trcl in same ch sp, 1 ch, *trcl, 1 ch, trcl, in next ch sp, 1 ch, repeat from * to end, ss into top of first tr to close round. (8 tr cluster pairs)
ROUND 4 Ss into next ch sp, 3 ch, 1 tr into ch sp, 1 ch, *trcl in next ch sp, 1 ch, repeat from * to end, ss into top of first tr to close round. (16 trcl)
ROUND 5 Ss into next ch sp, 3 ch, 1 tr into ch sp, 1 ch, trcl into same ch sp, 1 ch, *trcl, 1 ch, trcl in next ch sp, 1 ch, repeat from * to end, ss into top of first tr to close round. (16 tr cluster pairs)
ROUND 6 Ss into next ch sp, 3 ch, 1 tr into ch sp, 1 ch, *trcl in next ch sp, 1 ch, repeat from *

to end, ss into top of first tr to close round. (32 trcl)
ROUND 7 Ss into next ch sp, 3 ch, 1 tr into ch sp, 1 ch, trcl into same ch sp, 1 ch, trcl in next ch sp, ch 1 *trcl, 1 ch, trcl in next ch sp, 1 ch, trcl in next ch sp, 1 ch, repeat from * to end, ss into top of first tr to close round. (16 trcl and 16 tr cluster pairs)
ROUND 8 As round 6. (48 tr clusters)
ROUND 9 Ss into next ch sp, 5 ch, *1 dtr in next ch sp, 1 ch, repeat from * to end, join with a ss into fourth ch of 5 ch.
ROUND 10 Ss into next ch sp, 3 ch, 1 tr into ch sp, 1 ch, trcl into same ch sp, 1 ch, dtrcl in next ch sp, 1 ch, *trcl, 1 ch, trcl in next ch sp, 1 ch, dtrcl in next ch sp, 1 ch, repeat from * to end, ss into top of first tr to close round. (24 tr cluster pairs and 24 large tr clusters made)
ROUND 11 As round 6. (72 trcl)
ROUND 12 1 ch, *1 dc in top of trcl, 1 dc into ch sp, repeat from * to end, ss into 1 ch to close round.

Finishing
Weave in all ends securely on reverse.
Pin rug to a flat surface and spray lightly with water, shape to a flat circle, and leave to dry.
A non-slip backing can be sewn to the reverse of the rug, if desired.

>> This rug is made with Cygnet Seriously Chunky, 100g/48m/52yds, in Fawn (711).

The treble clusters and half treble clusters in this project create an attractive mesh pattern towards the outside of the rug and this contrasts well with the tighter stitches at the edge, and the nice neat finish given by the final row of double crochet.

Essential information

DIFFICULTY LEVEL Intermediate

SIZE 30 x 50cm (12 x 19¾in)

YARN Any DK wool will be suitable for this project

A x 4   **B** x 2

CROCHET HOOK 4mm hook

NOTIONS Yarn needle

TENSION 15 sts x 20 rows per 10cm (4in) square

Intarsia cushion

This simple bolster cushion is worked in two pieces and has an attractive diamond and stripe intarsia pattern. The pattern includes the option for a double-sided cushion or for stitching one side in plain crochet.

PROJECTS
For more cushion patterns
>> go to page 80

NOTE When changing yarn colour: with yarn A insert hook into next st, pull through a loop, change to yarn B, yrh and crochet both loops on hook. Work the next stitch in yarn B. Changing the yarn is completed in the final step of the previous stitch.

Cushion front

With yarn A, work 76 ch.
ROW 1 dc into second ch from hook, dc to end. (75sts)
ROW 2 1 ch, dc to end of row.
ROWS 3–9 Repeat row 2.
ROW 10 With yarn B, 1 ch, dc to end of row.
ROW 11 Repeat row 10.
ROW 12 With yarn A, 1 ch, dc to end of row.
ROW 13 Repeat row 12.
ROW 14–17 With yarn B, 1 ch, dc to end of row.
ROW 18–21 With yarn A, 1 ch, dc to end of row.
ROW 22 See chart, below right, for the colourwork intarsia design.

Working in intarsia and changing yarn colour before the final stage in the last stitch, with yarn A (referred to as A) 1 ch, 10 dc, yarn B (referred to as B) 1 dc, *A17 dc, B1 dc; repeat from * 2 more times, A10 dc.
ROW 23 Repeat row 22.
ROW 24 With A, 1 ch, 9 dc, B3 dc, *A15 dc, B3 dc; repeat from * two more times, A9 dc.
ROW 25 Repeat row 24.
ROW 26 With A, 1 ch, 8 dc, B2 dc, A1 dc, B2 dc, *A13 dc, B2 dc, A1 dc, B2 dc; repeat from * 2 more times, A8 dc.
ROW 27 Repeat row 26.
ROW 28 With A, 1 ch, 7 dc, B2 dc, A3 dc, B2 dc, *A5 dc, B1 dc, A5 dc, B2 dc, A3 dc, B2 dc; repeat from * 2 more times, A7 dc.
ROW 29 Repeat row 28.
ROW 30 With A, 1 ch, 6 dc, B2 dc, A2 dc, B1 dc, A2 dc, B2 dc, *A3 dc, B3 dc, A3 dc, B2 dc, A2 dc, B1 dc, A2 dc, B2 dc; repeat from * 2 more times, A6 dc.
ROW 31 Repeat row 30.
ROW 32 Repeat row 28.
ROW 33 Repeat row 32.
ROW 34 Repeat row 26.
ROW 35 Repeat row 34.
ROW 36 Repeat row 24.
ROW 37 Repeat row 36.

ROW 38 Repeat row 22.
ROW 39 Repeat row 38.
ROW 40 With A, 1 ch, dc to end of row.
ROWS 41–43 Repeat row 40.
ROWS 44–47 With B, 1 ch, dc to end of row.
ROWS 48–49 With A, 1 ch, dc to end of row.
ROWS 50–51 With B, 1 ch, dc to end of row.
ROWS 52–60 With A, 1 ch dc to end of row. Fasten off.

Cushion back

Repeat instructions for cushion front. For the plain version, work as follows: With yarn A, work 76 ch.
ROW 1 Dc into second ch from hook, dc to end of row. (75sts)
ROW 2 1 ch, dc to end of row.
ROWS 3–60 Repeat row 2. Fasten off.

Finishing

With right sides together, sew the cushion, leaving one shorter side open. Turn inside out and insert cushion pad. Either sew edges together or insert a zip.

<< This intarsia cushion is made with Rowan Pure Wool DK, 50g/130m/142yds, in A: Cream (00013) and B: Blue (00008).

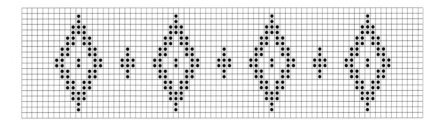

Circular cushion

The perfect project to practise working in the round, this cushion uses the simplest of stitches, a double crochet, and uses basic increasing to work flat circles. The circles are joined with a slip stitch crochet join.

PROJECTS
For more spiral patterns
>> go to page 70

Essential information

DIFFICULTY LEVEL Easy

SIZE Approx 35cm (13¾in) diameter

YARN You can use any aran weight yarn for this project, or a differing weight yarn to create a larger or smaller cushion cover

x 4

CROCHET HOOK 5mm hook

NOTIONS Stitch marker
Yarn needle
35cm (13¾in) round cushion pad

TENSION Exact tension is not essential

NOTE This cushion is worked in spirals. Do not join rounds, but place a marker at the first stitch of the round, moving it each round to mark the beginning of the round.

Pattern (make 2)

Work 2 ch and 6 dc into second ch from hook, join round with a ss to first st.

ROUND 1 1 ch, work 2 dc in each st around, do not join round, place marker. (12sts)

ROUND 2 *2 dc in next st, 1 dc in next st; rep from * to end. (18sts)

ROUND 3 *2 dc in next st, dc in next 2 sts; rep from * to end. (24sts)

ROUND 4 *2 dc in next st, dc in next 3 sts; rep from * to end. (30sts)

ROUND 5 *2 dc in next st, dc in next 4 sts; rep from * to end. (36sts)

ROUND 6 *2 dc in next st, dc in next 5 sts; rep from * to end. (42sts)

Continue in this way, working one extra st between increases for each round until you have worked 23 rounds and have 144 sts.

If you want a larger cushion, you can continue increasing in this way until the desired size is achieved.
Join round with a ss.
Fasten off yarn, weave in ends.

Finishing

Block pieces lightly. Arrange with wrong sides together, attach yarn to both pieces along edge, inserting the hook into a whole stitch of each circular piece. Work a slip stitch join around edge, trapping cushion pad in between when you have worked approximately halfway around the circumference.

>> This cushion is made with Sirdar Simply Recycled Aran, 50g/93m/102yds, in Canvas (11).

1 To make up the cushion, place the circles with wrong sides together and attach the yarn to the front piece with a ss.

2 Insert the hook through both loops of the next stitch of front piece and through both loops of the corresponding stitch on back. Yrh and pull through both stitches and loop on hook to make a ss.

3 When you are about halfway, stuff the cushion pad into the middle of the two rounds and continue slip stitching through both sides, joining the last stitch to the first with a slip stitch.

Chevron cushion

Working chevrons in stripes produces a striking fabric with little effort. Regular shaping creates the peaks and troughs, while the crisp cotton makes for well-defined zigzags.

PROJECTS
For more striped patterns
>> go to page 114

Essential information

DIFFICULTY LEVEL Easy

SIZE Approx 35 x 35cm (13¾ x 13¾in)

YARN Any DK yarn will substitute here. This uses cotton, but try a wool mix for a cosy alternative

A x 1　　B x 1　　C x 1

CROCHET HOOK 4mm hook

NOTIONS Yarn needle
35cm (13¾in) square cushion pad
2 black buttons

TENSION Exact tension is not essential

◀◀ This cushion is made with Twilleys Freedom Sincere DK, 50g/115m/126yds, in A: Snowdrop (600), B: Strawberry (623), and Rico Design Baby Cotton Soft DK, 50g/125m/137yds, in C: Black (27).

Pattern

With yarn A, work 73 ch.
ROW 1 1 dc into second ch from hook, 1 dc in each ch to end. Turn. (72sts)
ROW 2 1 ch, 1 dc into same st, 7 dc, miss next 2 dc, 7 dc, *2 dc in each of next 2 sts, 7 dc, miss next 2 dc, 7 dc; rep from * to last st, 2 dc in last st. Turn.
Row 2 forms pattern, rep for desired length of fabric, changing colour after every 4 rows in this order:
Yarn A
Yarn B
Yarn C
When fabric measures approx 75cm (29½in), ending with four rows of yarn A, fasten off yarn and weave in ends.

Finishing

Block piece lightly to shape.
Wrap piece around cushion pad, with an overlap halfway down the back of the pad. Ensure the starting edge of the piece is on top, and is overlapping the bottom of the piece. Sew up bottom two side seams of the cushion, then sew down the top two side seams, overlapping the bottom seam.
Fasten the opening of the cushion by sewing buttons on the bottom edge of the piece, corresponding to the missed dc sts next to the end of each point. These will form the buttonholes.

To ensure that the crochet doesn't stretch after the cushion pad is inserted, make a couple of overstitches underneath the buttons to join the two white zigzags on the flap and the backing of the cushion cover.

Mobile phone covers

Protect your phone from scratches with a rectangular cover made from double crochet. A speedy project to create, the crochet is simply sewn together to form a pouch.

PROJECTS
For more patterns with loops
>> go to page 120

Essential information

DIFFICULTY LEVEL Easy

SIZE Approx 7 x 13cm (2¾ x 5¼in)

YARN Any DK weight yarn will substitute – try to use a hardwearing yarn with some acrylic as the cover will get a lot of use

A x 1   **B** x 1   **C** small amount

CROCHET HOOK 4mm hook

NOTIONS Yarn needle
18mm (¾in) button to fasten

TENSION Exact tension is not essential

Pattern

With yarn A or B, work 30 ch.
ROW 1 1 dc into second ch from hook, 1 dc into each ch to end. Turn. (29 dc)
ROW 2 1 ch, 1 dc into each dc to end. Turn.

Plain cover

Repeat row 2 until the work is approx 12.5cm (5in).

Two-colour cover

Repeat row 2 until work is approx 10cm (4in). Change to second colour and repeat row 2 until work is approx 12.5cm (5in).

Both covers

BUTTON LOOP ROW 1 ch, 7 dc, 9 ch, dc back into last dc to form buttonhole loop, 1 dc in each dc to end.
Fasten off yarn, weave in ends.

Finishing

Block piece lightly.
Fold piece in half lengthways with loop at top, and sew up bottom and side seam with a mattress stitch.
Sew button to corresponding point along opposite edge to button loop. Insert your phone and fasten button.

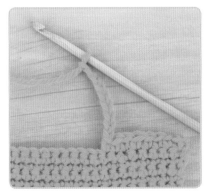

1 To make the button loop on the final row, dc across to placement of button loop, then chain 9 sts for the loop.

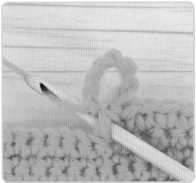

2 Work 1 dc into the same stitch at the bottom of the chain to close the loop, then dc to the end of the row.

>> This phone cover is made with Sirdar Snuggly DK, 50g/165m/179yds, in A: Pixie (415), B: Purple (197), and C: Spicy pink (350).

Button loops make great alternatives to buttonholes, and are ideal for phone covers where a single closure point is best. This loop uses just two crochet stitches – chain stitch and double crochet – worked into the final row of the phone cover.

Coin purses

These tiny projects are ideal for getting children into crochet. They are both worked in the round, in two different ways, to create small pouches for change.

PROJECTS

For more double crochet patterns
>> go to page 78

Essential information

DIFFICULTY LEVEL Easy

SIZE Round purse: approx 10cm (4in) diameter
Rectangular purses: approx 9 x 7cm (3½ x 2¾in)

YARN Any fine crochet thread will work

A x 3   B x 1   C x 1   D x 1   E x 3

CROCHET HOOK 2.5mm hook

NOTIONS Stitch marker
Yarn needle
9cm (3½in) zip for each purse
Bead (optional)

TENSION Exact tension is not essential

NOTE Purses are worked in spirals. Do not join rounds, but place a marker at first stitch of the round, moving it each round to mark the beginning of the next round.

Round purse

Make 2 ch and work 6 dc into second ch from hook, join round with a ss to first st.
ROUND 1 1 ch, work 2 dc in each dc around, do not join round, place marker. (12sts)
ROUND 2 (2 dc in next dc, 1 dc in next 1 dc) around. (18sts)
ROUND 3 (2 dc in next dc, 1 dc in next 2 dc) around. (24sts)
ROUND 4 (2 dc in next dc, 1 dc in next 3 dc) around. (30sts)
ROUND 5 (2 dc in next dc, 1 dc in next 4 dc) around. (36sts)
ROUND 6 (2 dc in next dc, 1 dc in next 5 dc) around. (42sts)
Continue in this way, working one extra st between increases in each round until you have worked 9 rounds and have 60 sts.
Work straight on these 60 sts for 7 rounds.
ROUND 17 (dc2tog, 1 dc in next 8 dc) around. (54sts)
Work 2 rounds straight.
ROUND 20 (dc2tog, 1 dc in next 7 dc) around. (48sts)
Work one round straight.
ROUND 22 (dc2tog, 1 dc in next 6 dc) around. (42sts)
Work two rounds straight.
Fasten off yarn and weave in ends.

Rectangular purse

Work 31 ch.
ROUND 1 3 dc into second ch from hook, 1 dc in each ch to last ch, 3 dc in last ch, turn work

180 degrees and work along other side of ch, working 1 dc into the bottom of each ch, do not join round.
ROUND 2 1 dc into each dc around.
Rep last round for desired height of purse, sample shown is 7cm (2¾in), changing colours for striping where desired.
Fasten off yarn and weave in ends.

Finishing

Sew zip into top of each purse. Make a tassel and attach it by inserting the strands through the zip hole, securing as normal and adding a bead, if desired.

When choosing a bead to attach to your zip pull, make sure that it's central hole is sufficiently large enough to thread the strands of DMC cotton through. Tie a knot right up close to the bead to secure.

>> These purses are made with DMC Petra Crochet Cotton Perle No. 3, 100g/280m/306yds, in A: Ecru, B: Kingfisher blue (53845), C: Pink (53805), D: Green (5907), and E: Blue (5798).

Baby bonnet

This bonnet has a simple construction – a rectangle folded and sewn to create a cute pixie point at the back. Create your own stripe sequence and textures by changing stitches for each stripe, as here, or use the same stitch all the way up.

PROJECTS
For more baby hat patterns
>>go to page 88

Essential information

DIFFICULTY LEVEL Easy

SIZE To fit a baby, aged 0-3 (3-6) months

YARN Any DK weight yarn will substitute here. Baby yarns are preferable for their softness and easy-to-wash fibres

A x 1   B x 1   C x 1

CROCHET HOOK 4mm hook

NOTIONS Yarn needle
15mm (½in) pink button

TENSION 18 dc to 10cm (4in) square

Pattern

With yarn A, work 56 (62) ch.
ROW 1 1 htr in third ch from hook, 1 htr in each ch to end. (54(60)htr)
ROW 2 2 ch, 1 htr in each st to end.
ROW 3 As row 2.
Change to yarn B.
ROW 4 1 ch, 1 dc in each st to end of row.
ROWS 5-7 As row 4.
Change to yarn C.
ROW 8 3 ch, 1 tr in each st to end of row.
ROW 9 As row 8.
ROWS 10-18 Rep rows 1–9 stripe sequence.
Change to yarn A.
ROWS 19-21 2 ch, 1 htr in each st to end.
Change to yarn B and work straight in dc until piece measures approx 15(16)cm/6(6¼)in.

Finishing

Fold piece in half lengthways to create the bonnet, sewing along top seam, which will become the back of bonnet, to close it.
ROUND 1 With yarn C, work 20 ch for chin strap, attach chain to bottom corner of the hat and work evenly in dc all around face opening, working 3 dc into corner sp to get round, then work in dc evenly along bottom of the bonnet for neck opening, join round with a ss.
ROUND 2 Work 1 dc into each ch of chin strap, working 3 dc into last ch, then turn work around 180 degrees and work back into unworked bottom loops of chain. Complete the face opening evenly in dc, then work (dc2tog, 1 dc) along the neck opening to decrease, work 1 dc into each dc along chin

Turn to pages 32–33 for seam techniques. Use the same coloured yarn for sewing up as the surrounding yarn of the seam, so that the stitching does not show.

strap, to centre dc of 3 dc, 3 ch, miss next dc, dc in each dc to end of chin strap. Fasten off yarn and weave in all ends.
Sew button to bottom corner of bonnet, corresponding to buttonhole of chin strap.

>> This bonnet is made with Debbie Bliss Baby Cashmerino, 50g/125m/137yds, in A: Ecru (101), B: Candy pink (006), and C: Hot pink (060).

Essential information

DIFFICULTY LEVEL Easy

SIZE To fit a child, aged 3-4 (4-5:5-6)

YARN Any DK weight yarn with a high merino wool content will achieve a similar effect

A x 2   **B** x 1

CROCHET HOOK 3.5mm hook

NOTIONS Yarn needle
Two circles cut from cardboard, with an outer diameter of 6cm (2¼in) and a ring cut from the middle with a diameter of 2.5cm (1in) to make the pompom

TENSION 19 sts x 8 rows per 10cm (4in)

SPECIAL ABBREVIATIONS
ADJUSTABLE RING: See p.122

Child's hat with earflaps

This simple and fun project will keep your little one cosy all winter. Worked in the round from the top, the hat uses half treble stitches to give warmth. The hat circumferences measure 45cm (17³/₄in), 47cm (18¹/₂in), and 48cm (19in).

PROJECTS

For more children's patterns
>> *go to pages 111 and 114*

Pattern

ROUND 1 Using the adjustable ring method of starting and yarn A, work 2 ch and then 6 htr into the ring. Gently close the ring and join into a round with a ss. (7sts)

ROUND 2 2 ch, 1 htr into same st, 2 htr into each st to end, join into a round with a ss. (14sts)

ROUND 3 2 ch, *2 htr into next st, 1 htr into next st; rep from * to last st, 2 htr into next st, join into a round with a ss. (21sts)

ROUND 4 2 ch, *2 htr into next st, 1 htr into each of next 2 sts; rep from * to last 2 sts, 2 htr into next st, 1 htr into next st, join into a round with a ss. (28sts)

Continue in this way, increasing 7 sts on each round until 9 rounds in total have been worked. (63sts)

ROUND 10 2 ch, 1 htr into each st to end, join into a round with a ss.

ROUND 11 2 ch, *2 htr into next st, 1 htr into each of next 8 sts; rep from * to last 8 sts, 2 htr into next st, 1 htr into each of next 7 sts, join into a round with a ss. (70sts)

<< This hat is made with Debbie Bliss Cashmerino DK, 50g/110m/120yds, in A: Apple (340002) and B: Candy pink (340006).

ROUND 12 2 ch, *2 htr into next st, 1 htr into each of next 9 sts; rep from * to last 9 sts, 2 htr into next st, 1 htr into each of next 8 sts, join into a round with a ss. (77sts)

ROUND 13 2 ch, 1 htr into each st to end, join into a round with a ss.

ROUND 14 2 ch, *2 htr into next st, 1 htr into each of next 10 sts; rep from * to last 10 sts, 2 htr into next st, 1 htr into each of next 9 sts, join into a round with a ss. (84sts)

MEDIUM AND LARGE SIZES ONLY

ROUND 15 2 ch, 1 htr into each st to end, join into a round with a ss.

ROUND 16 2 ch, *2 htr into next st, 1 htr into each of next 11 sts; rep from * to last 11 sts, 2 htr into next st, 1 htr into each of next 10 sts, join into a round with a ss. (91sts)

LARGE SIZE ONLY

ROUND 17 2 ch, 1 htr into each st to end, join into a round with a ss.

ROUND 18 2 ch, *2 htr into next st, 1 htr into each of next 12 sts; rep from * to last 12 sts, 2 htr into next st, 1 htr into each of next 11 sts, join into a round with a ss. (98sts)

ALL SIZES

Work straight (as per round 10) until the depth of the hat measures 15 (16:17)cm/ 6 (6¹/₄:6³/₄)in from the beginning.

NEXT ROUND With yarn B, 1 ch, 1 dc into each st to end, join into a round with a ss.

NEXT ROUND With yarn A, 2 ch, 1 htr into each st to end, join into a round with a ss.

NEXT ROUND With yarn B, 1 ch, 1 dc into each st to end, join into a round with a ss. Break off yarn B.

NEXT ROUND With yarn A, 2 ch, 1 htr into each st to end, join into a round with a ss. Break off yarn A.

Making the earflaps

Rejoin yarn A at 15 (15:16) sts after the end of the last round. 2 ch, 1 htr into each of the next 14 (15:16) sts. Turn.

ROW 1 2 ch, htr2tog, work 1 htr into each st to the last 2 sts, htr2tog. 12 (13:14) sts. Turn. Repeat row 1 until 2 (1:2) sts remain. Fasten off yarn. Make the second earflap on the other side of the hat to match.

Edging

Join yarn B to the end of the last complete round worked.

Work 1 ch. 1 dc into each st.

At the first earflap, work 2 dc into each end of row to the point of the earflap.

Work 26 ch, then turn and, starting from the third ch from hook, work 1 dc into each ch.

Work 2 dc into each end of row.

Work 1 dc into each st along the base of hat.

Work the second earflap in the same way as the first.

Work 1 dc into each st to the end of the round. Join with a ss. Fasten off yarn.

Finishing

Make a 6cm (2¹/₄in) pompom in yarn B and attach to the top of the hat. Weave in all ends.

Essential information

DIFFICULTY LEVEL Intermediate

SIZE To fit an adult female

YARN You can use any DK weight silk/wool blend for a similar effect

A x 1   B x 1   C x 1

CROCHET HOOK 4mm hook

NOTIONS Yarn needle

TENSION 8 bobbles per 10cm (4in)

SPECIAL ABBREVIATIONS

BEG BOBBLE: 3 ch, (yrh and insert hook in st, yrh and draw a loop through, yrh and draw through first 2 loops on hook) 3 times all in the same st, yrh and draw a loop through all 4 loops on hook.

BOBBLE STITCH: (yrh and insert hook in st, yrh and draw a loop through, yrh and draw through first 2 loops on hook) 4 times all in the same st, yrh and draw a loop through all 5 loops on hook.

DEC 1 BOBBLE: (yrh and insert hook in st, yrh and draw a loop through, yrh and draw through first 2 loops on hook) 4 times all in the same st, rep in next st, yrh and draw a loop through all 10 loops on hook.

CRAB STITCH: See p.82

Woman's beret

The beret is quick and easy to make and will make a perfect gift for a friend. The beret is worked in the round starting at the centre and then adding each row.

PROJECTS
For more crab stitch patterns
>> go to pages 82 and 111

Pattern

With yarn A, work 4 ch, ss in last ch from hook to form ring.

ROUND 1 3 ch, 11 tr into centre ring. (12sts)

ROUND 2 3 ch, (yrh and insert hook in first st, yrh and draw a loop through, yrh and draw through first 2 loops on hook) 3 times all in the same st, yrh and draw a loop through all 4 loops on hook, (counts as first bobble), *1 bobble in next st; rep from * 10 times, ss in top of 3 ch. Fasten off. (12 bobbles)

ROUND 3 With B, join yarn in any ch sp, beg bobble, 1 bobble in same sp, *2 bobbles in next ch sp; rep from * 10 times, ss in top of 3 ch. Fasten off. (24 bobbles)

ROUND 4 With C, join yarn in any ch sp, beg bobble, 1 ch, *1 bobble in next ch sp, 1 ch; rep from * 22 times, ss in top of 3 ch. Fasten off. (24 bobbles)

ROUND 5 With A, join yarn in any ch sp, beg bobble, 1 bobble in same ch sp, 1 bobble in next ch sp, *2 bobbles in next ch sp, 1 bobble in next ch sp; rep from * 10 times, ss in top of 3 ch. Fasten off. (36 bobbles)

ROUND 6 With B, join yarn in any ch sp, beg bobble, 1 ch, *1 bobble in next ch sp, 1 ch; rep

from * 34 times, ss in top of 3 ch. Fasten off. (36 bobbles)

ROUND 7 With C, join yarn in any ch sp, beg bobble, 1 bobble in same ch sp, 1 bobble in next 2-ch sp, *2 bobbles in next ch sp, 1 bobble in next 2-ch sp; rep from * 10 times, ss in top of 3 ch. Fasten off. (48 bobbles)

ROUND 8 With A, join yarn in any ch sp, beg bobble, 1 ch, *1 bobble in next ch sp, 1 ch; rep from * 46 times, ss in top of 3 ch. Fasten off. (48 bobbles)

ROUND 9 With B, join yarn in any ch sp, beg bobble, 1 bobble in same ch sp, 1 bobble in next 3-ch sp *2 bobbles in next ch sp, 1 bobble in next 3-ch sp; rep from * 10 times, ss in top of 3 ch. Fasten off. (60 bobbles)

ROUND 10 With C, join yarn in any ch sp, beg bobble, 1 ch, *1 bobble in next ch sp, 1 ch; rep from * 58 times, ss in top of 3 ch. Fasten off. (60 bobbles)

ROUND 11 With A, rep round 10.

ROUND 12 With B, rep round 10.

ROUND 13 With C, rep round 10.

ROUND 14 With A, join yarn in any ch sp, 3 ch, (yrh and insert hook in same ch sp, yrh and draw a loop through, yrh and draw through first 2 loops on hook) 3 times all in the same ch sp, (yrh and insert hook in next ch sp, yrh and draw a loop through, yrh and draw through first 2 loops on hook) 4 times all in the same ch sp, yrh and draw a loop through all 10 loops on hook, (dec 1 bobble), 1 ch, (1 bobble in next ch sp, 1 ch) 3 times, *dec 1 bobble, 1 ch (1 bobble in next ch sp, 1 ch) 3 times; rep from * 10 times, ss in top of 3 ch. Fasten off. (48 bobbles)

ROUND 15 With B, join yarn in any ch sp, beg bobble, 1 ch, *1 bobble in next ch sp, 1 ch; rep

The lovely bobble stitches used in this hat make it a very tactile and attractive project.

from * 46 times, ss in top of 3 ch. Fasten off. (48 bobbles)

ROUND 16 With C, join yarn in any ch sp, 3 ch, (yrh and insert hook in same ch sp, yrh and draw a loop through, yrh and draw through first 2 loops on hook) 3 times all in the same ch sp, (yrh and insert hook in next ch sp, yrh and draw a loop through, yrh and draw through first 2 loops on hook) 4 times all in the same ch sp, yrh and draw a loop through all 10 loops on hook, (dec 1 bobble), 1 ch, (1 bobble in next ch sp, 1 ch) twice, *dec 1 bobble, 1 ch (1 bobble in next ch sp, 1 ch) twice; rep from * 10 times, ss in top of 3 ch. (36 bobbles)

ROUND 17 With A, join yarn in any ch sp, 1 ch, work 1 dc in the top of each bobble and each 1 ch around, ss in top of ch. (72sts)

ROUNDS 18–19 Repeat round 17.

ROUND 20 1 ch, work in crab stitch around, ss in ch.

Fasten off, weave in ends.

Broomstick lace shawl

What better accessory for a wedding or summer party in the garden than this delicate, threadlike shawl? Crocheted with a long broomstick and using gossamer fine yarn, the stunning result hides how easy it is to make.

PROJECTS
For more openwork patterns
>> go to page 50

Essential information

DIFFICULTY LEVEL Easy

SIZE Approx 60 x 150cm (23½ x 59in)

YARN Any lace weight mohair yarn will give a similar effect. This pattern is also suitable for using with any DK yarn for a more solid shawl. Non-fluffy yarns will produce a robust shawl

x 5

CROCHET HOOK 4.5mm hook

NOTIONS 20mm x 35 or 40cm (8 x 14 or 15¾in) long broomstick or knitting needle
Yarn needle

TENSION 6 groups of 4 loops (24 dc) and 4 rows to 10cm (4in)

NOTE The shawl is a straight piece of broomstick crochet, but half of it is worked on one side of the foundation row of double crochet, referred to here as the "spine", and half of it is worked on the other side. This gives a symmetrical look to the finished shawl. If you find it hard to insert the hook into the top of the dc to put the next loop on the broomstick, use a smaller, pointed-ended hook – remember to use the 4.5mm hook to work the dc sts.

Construction pattern

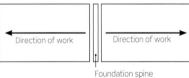

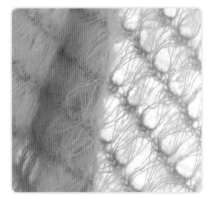

Work the foundation row of double crochet into the back bump only of the initial chain, to provide balanced loops to work each side of the shawl outwards, from the centre back foundation "spine".

Foundation spine and first side
Work 144 ch making sure they are kept nice and loose. Leave a long tail in case you miscount and need to make a few extra chains to get the right number of stitches on the foundation row.
Insert hook under back bump only of first ch, 1 dc. Insert hook in same way, 1 dc in each ch to end. (144 dc)

Pattern row
Pick up a loop onto the broomstick in each dc across. (144 loops)
Take off loops in groups of 4, placing 4 dc in each group. (144 dc = 36 groups)
Rep pattern row for half of required length.
Fasten off.

Second side
Join yarn to end of initial spine of dc farthest away from the tail of yarn and work pattern row as for first side.

Finishing
Weave in all ends.
Avoid heavy blocking of this shawl or you will flatten the beautiful, fluffy texture of the yarn. Pin out to the required size, lightly spritz with water, and allow to dry naturally.

>> This shawl is made with Rowan Kidsilk Haze, 25g/210m/230yds, in Meadow (581).

Ladies' wrist warmers

These vibrant and practical wrist warmers have a pretty, three-dimensional texture created by puff stitches and a crochet rib using raised trebles.

PROJECTS
For child's mittens
>> go to page 98

Essential information

DIFFICULTY LEVEL Intermediate

SIZE Approx 20 (22:24)cm/8 (8¾:9½)in

YARN Any DK weight yarn will substitute here

x 2

CROCHET HOOK 3.5mm hook

TENSION 18 tr to 10cm (4in) square

NOTIONS Yarn needle

SPECIAL ABBREVIATIONS

RTRF: raised treble front: At the front of the work, yrh, insert hook from right to left, around the post of the treble stitch on the previous row, yrh, draw through, yrh, draw through 2 loops on hook, yrh, draw through last 2 loops on hook, therefore making a treble stitch.

RTRB: raised treble back. At the back of the work, yrh, insert hook from right to left, around the post of the treble stitch on the previous row, yrh, draw through, yrh, draw through 2 loops on hook, yrh, draw through last 2 loops on hook, therefore making a treble stitch.

PUFF STITCH: *yrh, insert into st, yrh and draw loop through the stitch, drawing loop up to the height of the sts in the row; rep from * 4 times

These wrist warmers are made from two basic rectangles sewn together with gaps left for thumb holes. Turn to pages 32–33 for details about seams.

into the same st. 9 loops on hook, yrh, and draw loop through all loops on hook. Puff completed.

Pattern

Work 32 (35:40) ch.
ROW 1 1 tr into third ch from hook and into each ch to end. Turn. (29 (33:37)sts)
ROW 2 3 ch (counts as first RtrB), *1 RtrF, 1 RtrB; rep from * to end of row.
ROW 3 3 ch (counts as first RtrF), *1 RtrB, 1 RtrF; rep from * to end of row.
Rep last two rows until rib measures approx 8cm (3in), or desired length.

Right glove

ROW 1 (RS) 2 ch, 1 htr in each st to end, turn.
Rep last row twice more.
ROW 4 3 ch, (1 puff, 1 tr) 8 times, htr to end of row, turn.

Rep row 1 three times.
ROW 8 3 ch, (1 tr, 1 puff) 7 times, htr to end of row, turn.
Rep row 1 three times.
ROWS 12–18 As rows 4–11.
ROW 19 As row 1.
Fasten off yarn, leaving long end for sewing up seam.

Left glove

ROW 1 (RS) 2 ch, 1 htr in each st to end, turn.
Rep last row twice more.
ROW 4 3 ch, htr to last 16 sts, (1 puff, 1 tr) 8 times, turn.
Rep row 1 three times.
ROW 8 3 ch, htr to last 15 sts, (1 puff, 1 tr) 7 times, 1 tr into last st, turn.
Rep row 1 three times.
ROWS 12–18 As rows 4–11.
ROW 19 As row 1.
Fasten off yarn, leaving long end for sewing up seam.

Finishing

Fold each glove in half lengthways so that right sides face each other, then sew up side seam 5cm (2in) down from top, fasten off yarn, and reattach approx 6cm (2½in) further down the seam, to allow space for thumb, checking that the distance is correct to fit your hand. Sew up remainder of seam down to bottom of rib.

>> These wrist warmers are made with Artesano DK, 50g/100m/109yds, in Belize (1492).

Tweed stitch cowl

This warm and cosy cowl is made in the round using the shape of a Möebius strip. By making one twist, the loop appears never-ending and each round of crochet increases both the top and the bottom of the piece.

PROJECTS

For more winter warmer patterns
>> *go to page 106*

Essential information

DIFFICULTY LEVEL Easy

SIZE 92 x 18cm (36 x 7in)

YARN Any aran weight yarn with high wool content will produce a similar effect

x 4

CROCHET HOOK 5.5mm hook

NOTIONS Stitch marker
Yarn needle

TENSION 16 sts x 18 rows per 10cm (4in)

Pattern

Work 148 ch.

FOUNDATION ROW Starting in the third ch from hook, *1 dc into next st, 1 ch, miss next st; rep from * to last st, 1 dc into last st. Join with a ss into the last ch from hook (i.e. the base of the first st), making 1 twist (which means that round 1 will be worked in the base of the sts on the foundation row).

Mark the first st with the stitch marker or safety pin. (This is purely to help you see easily where the round has started; the double-sided nature of the cowl and the fabric can sometimes make this tricky.)

ROUND 1 1 ch, *work 1 dc into the ch sp on the row below, 1 ch, miss next st; rep from * to end, join with a ss.

ROUND 2 3 ch, *miss next st, work 1 dc into the ch sp on the row below, 1 ch; rep from * to last st, work 1 dc into the last st, join with a ss. Repeat these 2 rows 7 more times (16 rows in total).

Fasten off, weave in ends.

Tweed stitch is an easy crochet stitch that is also known as seed stitch. It creates a dense-textured fabric, which is ideal for a winter warmer.

>> This cowl is made with Rowan Felted Tweed Aran, 50g/87m/95yds, in Plum (731).

Child's mittens with string

Simple stitches in bright colours create the perfect accessory for little boys or girls. Constructed in spirals of double crochet, these mittens work up in next to no time and are ideal for beginners.

PROJECTS

For more beginner patterns
>> go to pages 58 and 78

Essential information

DIFFICULTY LEVEL Easy

SIZE To fit a child, aged 6–10 years

YARN You can use any soft 4-ply to DK weight yarn with a synthetic content for durability to achieve a similar effect

A x 1   B x 1   C x 1

CROCHET HOOK 3.25mm hook

NOTIONS Stitch marker
Yarn needle

TENSION Exact tension is not essential

NOTE You may find it useful to mark the last st of first 4 rounds with a stitch marker. Do not join rounds, but place a marker at the first stitch of the round, moving it up as each round is completed to mark the beginning of each round.

Pattern (make 2)

With yarn A, work 4 ch, ss in first ch to form a ring.
ROUND 1 6 dc into ring. (6sts)
ROUND 2 2 dc in each st. (12sts)
ROUND 3 *1 dc in first st, 2 dc in next st, rep from * to end of round. (18sts)
ROUND 4 *1 dc in next 2 sts, 2 dc in next st, rep from * to end of round. (24sts)
ROUND 5 ONWARDS Continue to work in dc until piece measures 8cm (3in).

The joining string is 100 chain stitches long, but you can lengthen or shorten it to suit the height of your child simply by adding or omitting stitches.

Thumb opening

NEXT ROUND 6 ch, miss 6 dc, dc to end of round (this is first of 6 ch).
NEXT ROUND 1 dc in each of 6 ch, dc to end. Work dc in each st for 3 further rounds. Fasten off A.
Join B into any dc, work 2 rounds of dc in B, fasten off B.
Join C into any dc, work 2 rounds of dc in C, fasten off C.
Rejoin A to any dc, work 3 rounds of dc in A. Fasten off yarn, weave in ends.

Thumb

Join A to any point around thumb opening. Work 12 dc evenly around gap.
Working in dc, continue to work in a spiral until thumb measures 3.5cm ($1^3/_8$in).
NEXT ROUND Dc2tog to end of round. (6sts)
Cut off yarn leaving a long tail, thread tail onto a yarn needle then thread through remaining stitches, pull tight, and fasten off. Join A into a dc on last round of first mitten, make 100 ch (or to desired length), ss into any st on last round of second mitten. Fasten off yarn, weave in ends.

>> These mittens are made with Debbie Bliss Baby Cashmerino, 50g/125m/137yds, in A: Sky (340032), B: Rose (340054), and C: Lime (340018).

Essential information

DIFFICULTY LEVEL Easy/Intermediate

SIZE To fit a child, aged 3–6 months
For a smaller shoe, see caption on page 103

YARN You can use any DK weight yarn with some
cotton content for structure

A x 1   **B** x 1

CROCHET HOOK 3.5mm hook

NOTIONS Yarn needle
2 small pieces of Velcro®
Sewing needle and thread

SPECIAL ABBREVIATIONS
RAISED DOUBLE CROCHET BACK (RDCB):
At the back of the work, insert hook from right to
left, around the post of the dc on the previous
row, yrh, draw through, yarn around hook, draw
through 2 loops on hook, therefore making a dc.

TENSION 10 sts per 5cm (2in)

Baby boy's booties

These booties are worked in a round, with a raised contrast colour strip separating sole from sides and a chunky strap to keep them on tiny feet. Using Velcro® to fasten makes them really easy to put on and take off, too!

PROJECTS
For more shoe patterns
>> go to page 102

For a rigid shoe, use a cotton-based yarn that will create a stiff fabric. For a softer feel, try a pure merino yarn. Refer to page 30 for instructions on how to work double crochet increases.

<< These booties are made with Rowan Wool Cotton DK, 50g/113m/124yds, in A: Ship Shape (955) and B: Clear (941).

Pattern

Measure the length of the sole after completing round 7 – it should be approx 10–11cm (4–4¼in).

Sole

With yarn A, work 9 ch, starting in second ch from hook.

ROUND 1 7 dc, 3 dc in next st, rotate through 180 degrees and continue along the back loop of the chains, 6 dc, 2 dc in last st, ss in first st. (18sts)

ROUND 2 1 ch, 1 dc inc, 6 dc, 3 htr inc, 6 dc, dc inc in each of last 2 dc, ss in first st. (24sts)

ROUND 3 1 ch, 1 dc, 1 dc inc, 6 dc, *1 htr, 1 htr inc; rep from * 2 more times, 6 dc, **1 dc, 1 dc inc; rep from ** 1 more time, ss in first st. (30sts)

ROUND 4 1 ch, 2 dc, 1 dc inc, 6 dc, *2 htr, 1 htr inc; rep from * 2 more times, 6 dc, **2 dc, 1 dc inc; rep from ** 1 more time, ss in first st. (36sts)

ROUND 5 1 ch, 3 dc, 1 dc inc, 6 dc, *3 htr, 1 htr inc; rep from * 2 more times, 6 dc, **3 dc, 1 dc inc; rep from ** 1 more time, ss in first st. (42sts)

ROUND 6 1 ch, 4 dc, 1 dc inc, 6 dc, *4 htr, 1 htr inc; rep from * 2 more times, 6 dc, **4 dc, 1 dc inc; rep from ** 1 more time, ss in first st. (48sts)

ROUND 7 Change to yarn B, 1 ch, 5 dc, 1 dc inc, 6 dc, *5 htr, 1 htr inc; rep from * 2 more times, 6 dc, **5 dc, 1 dc inc; rep from ** 1 more time, ss in first st. (54sts)

Sides

ROUND 8 1 ch, 54 rdcb, ss into first st.
ROUND 9 1 ch, 54 rdcb, ss into first st.
ROUND 10 Change to yarn A, 1 ch, 54 dc, ss into first st.
ROUND 11 1 ch, 54 dc, ss into first st.
ROUND 12 1 ch, 13 dc, *htr2tog, 3 htr; rep from * 3 more times, htr2tog, 17 dc, dc2tog. (48sts)
ROUND 13 1 ch, 13 dc, *htr2tog, 2 htr; rep from * 3 more times, htr2tog, 15 dc, dc2tog. (42sts)
ROUND 14 1 ch, 13 dc, *htr2tog, 1 htr; rep from * 3 more times, htr2tog, 13 dc, dc2tog. (36sts)
ROUND 15 1 ch, 13 dc, 5 htr2tog, 13 dc, ss into first st. (31sts)
Fasten off.

Straps

With yarn A, work 9 ch, starting in second ch from hook.

ROW 1 8 dc. (8sts)
ROWS 2–12 Turn work, ch 1, 8 dc.
ROW 13 Dc2tog, 4 dc, dc2tog. (6sts)
ROW 14 Dc2tog, 2 dc, dc2tog. (4sts)
ROW 15 2 dc2tog. (2sts) Fasten off.
Add some surface crochet stripes in chain stitch on the rounded edge for decoration, in yarn B.

Finishing

Sew the straps onto the shoes. Cut two small squares of Velcro® and sew on to secure the rounded edge of the strap down.
Weave in loose ends.

Baby girl's booties

These little shoes would make the perfect baby shower gift. They are worked up in a single piece in a round, from the middle of the sole and up to the sides, with the strap added after. A contrasting colour trim and a button complete the look.

PROJECTS

For more patterns in the round
>> go to pages 72 and 90

For a smaller shoe to fit a 0–3 month old, measuring 9 x 6cm (3½ x 2½in), swap the htr stitches for dc stitches where pattern indicates. Alternatively, stop making the sole part when you get to the length you need, and go on to make sides, matching the number of decreases in each round.

Pattern

After completing round 7, measure the length of the sole – it should be approx 10–11cm (4–4¼in) long. Ss into starting ch at end of each round.

Sole

With yarn A, work 9 ch, starting in second ch from hook.
ROUND 1 7 dc, 3 dc in next st, do not turn, continue in back loops of foundation ch, 6 dc, 2 dc in last st, ss in first st. (18sts)
ROUND 2 1 ch, 2 dc in next st, 6 dc, 2 htr in next st 3 times, 6 dc, 2 dc in next 2 sts, ss in first st. (24sts)
ROUND 3 1 ch, 1 dc, 2 dc in next st, 6 dc, *1 htr, 2 htr in next st; rep from * 2 more times, 6 dc, **1 dc, 2 dc in next st; rep from ** 1 more time, ss in first st. (30sts)
ROUND 4 1 ch, 2 dc, 2 dc in next st, 6 dc, *2 htr, 2 htr in next st; rep from * 2 more times, 6 dc, **2 dc, 2 dc in next st; rep from ** 1 more time, ss in first st. (36sts)
ROUND 5 1 ch, 3 dc, 2 dc in next st, 6 dc, *3 htr, 2 htr in next st; rep from * 2 more times, 6 dc, **3 dc, 2 dc in next st; rep from ** 1 more time, ss in first st. (42sts)
ROUND 6 1 ch, 4 dc, 2 dc in next st, 6 dc, *4 htr, 2 htr in next st; rep from * 2 more times, 6 dc, **4 dc, 2 dc in next st; rep from ** 1 more time, ss in first st. (48sts)
ROUND 7 1 ch, 5 dc, 2 dc in next st, 6 dc, *5 htr, 2 htr in next st; rep from * 2 more times, 6 dc, **5 dc, 2 dc in next st; rep from ** 1 more time, ss in first st. (54sts)

Sides

ROUND 8 2 ch (counts as first st), 53 htr, ss into second ch (for smaller shoe size, replace all htr stitches with dc stitches). (54sts)
ROUND 9 2 ch (counts as first st), 12 htr, htr2tog, 17 htr, htr2tog, 15 htr, htr2tog, 3 htr, ss into second ch. (51sts)
ROUND 10 2 ch (counts as first st), 12 htr, htr2tog, 16 htr, htr2tog, 14 htr, htr2tog, 2 htr, ss into second ch. (48sts)
ROUND 11 2 ch (counts as first st), 12 htr, htr3tog, 14 htr, htr3tog, 12 htr, htr2tog, 1 htr, ss into second ch. (43sts)
ROUND 12 1 ch (does not count as st), 13 dc, dc3tog, 12 dc, dc3tog, 10 dc, dc2tog, ss into first st. (38sts)
Fasten off.

Straps

For the right shoe, count 3 sts from the left side dc3tog from row 12, then attach yarn A. For the left shoe, count 1 st from the right side dc3tog from row 12, then attach yarn A.
ROW 1 1 ch, 2 dc. (2sts)
ROWS 2–12 Turn work, 1 ch, 2 dc.
ROW 13 8 ch, ss into last st to make a loop.
Fasten off.

Trim

With yarn B, work an even trim of reverse double crochet, or crab stitch, (see p.82) along the top edge of the shoe, going all around the strap.

Button (make 2)

With yarn B, make an adjustable ring (see p.122).
ROUND 1 6 dc into the ring, pull ring tight. (6sts)
ROUND 2 2 dc in each st. (12sts)
ROUND 3 Dc in each st.
ROUND 4 Dc2tog across all sts. (6sts)
Sew up button opening and sew to shoes. Weave in loose ends.

>> These booties are made with Rowan Wool Cotton DK, 50g/113m/124yds, in A: Flower (943) and B: Tender (951).

Essential information

DIFFICULTY LEVEL Easy

SIZE To fit a baby, aged 3–6 months

YARN Any DK weight yarn with some cotton content for added structure will be perfect here

A x 1   B x 1

CROCHET HOOK 3.5mm hook

NOTIONS Yarn needle

TENSION 10 sts x 5cm (2in)

SPECIAL ABBREVIATIONS

CRAB STITCH: Means simply working dc in reverse, working round the row, or round in this case, from left to right, instead of right to left. After completing a row of dc, do not turn the work around; work 1 ch, *insert the hook into the next stitch to the right, not in the stitch you just completed, but the next one. Draw a loop through. Yrh as normal and pull through both loops on the hook; rep from * across row.

Essential information

DIFFICULTY LEVEL Intermediate

SIZE To fit an adult male, UK shoe sizes 9-11

YARN You can use any DK weight wool/ acrylic blend yarn to achieve a similar effect

A x 1   **B** x 1

CROCHET HOOK 2.5mm and 3mm hooks

TENSION 19 sts x 14 rows per 10cm (4in)

NOTIONS 2 stitch markers
Yarn needle

SPECIAL ABBREVIATIONS

LHTR: linked half treble. On starting st, insert hook into second ch of starting ch, yrh, draw through, insert hook into st, yrh, draw through st, yrh, draw through all loops on hook. For each st after that as follows: insert hook into horizontal bar in st before, yrh, draw through, insert hook into st, yrh, draw through st, yrh, draw through all loops on hook.

LHTR2TOG: linked half treble 2 together. Insert hook into horizontal bar in st before, yrh, draw through, insert hook into next st, yrh, draw through st, insert hook into next st, yrh, draw through st, yrh, draw through all loops on hook.

Men's chunky socks

These cosy socks are made in the round, worked from the cuff down, with a contrasting colour used on the ribbing, heel, and toe, and worked in stripes to add extra detailing.

PROJECTS
For more double crochet patterns
>> go to pages 72 and 78

Socks (make 2)
Adjust the size by adding or subtracting stitches in the round to change the circumference, or by working the foot longer or shorter to adjust the length.

Cuff ribbing (worked sideways)
With 2.5mm hook and yarn B, 1 htr in each ch to end, turn. (12sts)
ROW 2 1 htr TBL in each st to end, turn.
Rep row 2 a further 46 times. (48 rows)
Using ss all along row, join first row to last row to form a large ring.

Cuff to heel
Turn ribbing 90 degrees, so you are working into the sides of the rows on the cuff.
ROUND 1 With 3mm hook and yarn A, 2 ch, 1 lhtr in each row side to end, change to yarn B, join, place stitch marker to indicate end of round. (48sts)
ROUND 2 2 ch, lhtr in each st to end, change to yarn A, join.
ROUND 3 2 ch, lhtr2tog, lhtr in each st to 2sts from marker, lhtr2tog, change to yarn B, join. (46sts)

ROUND 4 Rep round 2, change to yarn A.
ROUND 5 Rep round 2, change to yarn B.
ROUND 6 Rep round 3. (44sts)
ROUND 7 Rep round 2, change to yarn A.
ROUND 8 Rep round 2, do not join.
From now on, work in continuous rounds throughout.
ROUND 9 1 lhtr, lhtr2tog, lhtr in each st to 2 sts from marker, lhtr2tog. (42sts)
Work straight in continuous rounds of lhtr until sock measures 17cm (6³⁄₄in) from cuff edge.

Heel
ROW 1 22 lhtr (do NOT fasten off yarn A, as you will pick this up again later on the foot). With yarn B, 20 dc, turn.
ROW 2 1 ch, 1 dc in each dc to end, turn.
Rep row 2 until heel measures 6cm (2¹⁄₂in).

Turn the heel
ROW 1 1 ch, 12 dc, dc2tog, 1 dc, turn.
ROW 2 1 ch, 6 dc, dc2tog, 1 dc, turn.
ROW 3 Dc to 1 st from end of prev row, dc2tog (your second st of the dc2tog will be the next dc which is 2 rows below), 1 dc, turn.
Rep row 3 until you reach the end of the heel stitches, there will be no dc after the dc2tog at the end of your last 2 rows. (12sts)
Fasten off.

Foot
ROUND 1 With yarn A, left in place at beginning of heel, 2 ch, work 8 lhtr evenly up the side of the heel, 1 lhtr in each of the sts from the heel turn and 8 lhtr evenly placed down the other side of the heel flap; place

marker, work lhtr in each lhtr across the front of foot, place marker. (50sts)
You are now working in continuous rounds of lhtr again.
ROUND 2 Lhtr2tog, 1 lhtr, lhtr2tog, 18 lhtr, lhtr2tog, 1 lhtr, lhtr2tog, slip marker, lhtr in each st to next marker. (46sts)
ROUND 3 Lhtr2tog, 1 lhtr, lhtr2tog, 14 lhtr, lhtr2tog, 1 lhtr, lhtr2tog, remove marker, lhtr in each st to next marker. (42sts)
ROUND 4 Lhtr in each st to end of round.
Work in continuous rounds of lhtr until sock measures 25cm (10in) from heel.

Toe
ROUND 1 With yarn B, 21 dc, place marker, dc to end of round.
ROUND 2 Dc2tog, *dc to 2 sts from marker, dc2tog**, slip marker, dc2tog, rep from * between * and **. (38sts)
Rep round 2, 6 times. (14sts)
Fasten off, leaving a long end.

Finishing
Turn sock inside out and using the end left from fastening off, ss across both thicknesses of toe sts to seam together. Weave in ends.

Essential information

DIFFICULTY LEVEL Intermediate

SIZE To fit an adult female, UK shoe sizes 4–7

YARN You could substitute any DK weight sock yarn for this project, preferably with nylon

x 1

CROCHET HOOK 2.5mm and 3mm hooks

NOTIONS 2 stitch markers
Yarn needle

TENSION 23 sts x 22 rows per 10cm (4in)

Ladies' ankle socks

These pretty, comfortable socks, are worked in the round from the cuff down, using an alternating pattern of double crochet and treble crochet stitches. The tip of the toe and the heel are reinforced by using double crochet.

PROJECTS

For more double crochet patterns
>> go to pages 60 and 125

Pattern (make 2)

Work the cuff-ribbing sideways.

Cuff-ribbing (worked sideways)

With 2.5mm hook, work 10 ch.
ROW 1 1 htr in third ch from hook, 1 htr in each ch to end, turn. (8sts)
ROW 2 1 htr TBL in each st to end, turn.
Rep row 2 a further 28 times. (30 rows)
Using ss all along row, join first row to last row to form a large ring.

Cuff to heel

Turn ribbing 90 degrees, so you are working into the sides of the rows on the cuff.
ROUND 1 With 3mm hook, work 45 dc evenly around the cuff, place marker to indicate end of round.
You are now working in continuous rounds.
ROUND 2 *1 dc, 1 tr, rep from * to marker, 1 dc.
ROUND 3 *1 tr, 1 dc, rep from * to marker, 1 tr.
Rep rounds 2 and 3 until sock measures 19cm (7¹/₂in), making sure to end on a round 3.

Heel

ROW 1 22 dc, turn.
ROW 2 1 ch, 22 dc, turn.

Work in rows of dc until heel flap measures 5cm (2in).

Turn the heel

ROW 1 1 ch, 13 dc, dc2tog, 1 dc, turn.
ROW 2 6 dc, dc2tog, 1 dc, turn.
ROW 3 Dc to 1 st from end of prev row, dc2tog (your second st of the dc2tog will be the next dc, which is 2 rows below), 1 dc, turn.
Rep row 3, 5 times. (14sts)

Foot

ROUND 1 14 dc, evenly work 10 dc in side of heel rows, place marker, 1 dc, *1 tr, 1 dc, rep from * across to other side of heel, 1 tr, place marker, evenly work 12 dc into sides of heel rows, place marker to indicate end of round. (59sts)
ROUND 2 20 dc, (dc2tog) twice, 1 tr, *1 dc, 1 tr, rep from * to marker, 1 dc, (dc2tog) twice, dc to end marker. (55sts)
ROUND 3 (1 dc, 1 tr) 9 times, dc2tog, tr2tog, 1 dc, *1 tr, 1 dc, rep from * to marker, 1 dc, tr2tog, dc2tog, (1 tr, 1 dc) twice, 1 tr. (51sts)
ROUND 4 (1 tr, 1 dc) 8 times, tr2tog, dc2tog, 1 tr, *1 dc, 1 tr, rep from * to marker, 1 tr, dc2tog, tr2tog, (1 dc, 1 tr) twice. (47sts)
Remove all but ending marker.
ROUND 5 *1 dc, 1 tr, rep from * to last st, 1 dc.
ROUND 6 *1 tr, 1 dc, rep from * to last st, 1 tr.
Rep last 2 rounds until sock measures 23cm (9in).

Toe

ROUND 1 16 dc, dc2tog, place marker, 1 dc, dc2tog, 23 dc, place marker, dc to end of round. (46sts)
ROUND 2 *dc to 3 sts from marker, dc2tog,

Adjust the size of these socks by adding or subtracting stitches in multiples of two, in the round, to change the foot circumference, or by working the foot longer or shorter to adjust the length.

1 dc, slip marker (put it into the new loop on your hook to mark the start of the next round), 1 dc, dc2tog, rep from * once, dc to end of round. (42sts)
Rep round 2, 3 times. (On the last round there will be no dc after the last dc2tog). (30sts)
Remove end marker.
ROUND 3 *dc to 3 sts from marker, dc2tog, 1 dc, slip marker, 1 dc, dc2tog, rep from * once. (26sts)
ROUND 4 Rep round 3. (22sts)
Fasten off, leaving a long end.

Finishing

Turn sock inside out and using the end left from fastening off, ss across both thicknesses of toe sts to seam together. Weave in ends.

Cropped sweater

This pretty top is a great addition to a summer wardrobe. Lacy, with three-quarter length sleeves, it's perfect for layering on cold days. Worked flat in four pieces, the sweater is seamed together at the end.

PROJECTS
For more cluster patterns
>> *go to page 74*

Essential information

DIFFICULTY LEVEL Intermediate

SIZE To fit an adult female, S (M:L)

YARN You can use any DK weight alpaca or wool yarn here. This has a slight sparkle, which you could recreate with Lurex®

x 4 (4:5)

CROCHET HOOK 3.5mm hook

NOTIONS Safety pins
Yarn needle

TENSION 16 sts x 20 rows per 10cm (4in)

SPECIAL ABBREVIATIONS

2TR-CL: 2 treble crochet cluster. Yrh, insert in ch sp below, yrh, draw through, yrh, draw through 2 loops, yrh, insert in next ch sp, yrh, draw through, yrh, draw through remaining 3 loops.
UPTURNED V STITCH: ROW 1 (working into row of dc) 3 ch, *2tr-cl (see above) (work first tr into first dc, miss 1 dc, work second tr in next dc), 1 ch, rep from * to end, 1 tr in last st.
ROW 2 3 ch, 2tr-cl across row.
Rep row 2 for pattern.

The main body of the sweater is made up of a simple-to-follow lace repeat, with double crochet worked into the edges. Turn to pages 56–57 for more information about simple lace techniques, and page 58 for lace and filet patterns.

Pattern

The following pattern will fit three bust sizes: small: 81cm (32in), medium: 91cm (36in), and large: 101cm (40in).

Front

Work 77 (85:92) ch.
ROW 1 1 dc in second ch from hook, 1 dc in each ch to end, turn. (76(84:91)sts)
ROW 2 1 ch, 1 dc in each st to end, turn.
Rep row 2 a further 7 times.

SMALL AND LARGE SIZES ONLY
ROW 10 1 ch, 4 (1) dc, *2 dc in next st, 2 dc, rep from * to end. (100(121)sts)

MEDIUM SIZE ONLY
ROW 10 1 ch, 6 dc, 2 dc in next st, 2 dc, *2 dc in next st, 1 dc, 2 dc in next st, 2 dc, rep from * to end. (115sts)

ALL SIZES
ROW 11 Work row 1 of Upturned V Stitch pattern. (33 (38:40) 2tr-cl)
ROW 12 Work row 2 of Upturned V Stitch pattern.
Rep row 12 until piece measures 31 (32:33)cm /12¼ (12½:13)in.

Shape the armholes

ROW 1 *ss into next 2tr-cl, ss in ch-1 sp, rep from * once, 3 ch, work row 2 of Upturned V Stitch pattern across to third from last ch sp (leaving 2 2tr-cl unworked). (29 (34:36) 2tr-cl)
ROW 2 Work row 2 of Upturned V Stitch pattern.
Rep row 2 until armhole measures 14 (15:16cm/5½ (6:6¼)in from armhole shaping, ending on WS row.

Shape the neck

LEFT SIDE
ROW 1 (RS) 3 ch, *2tr-cl, 1 ch, rep from * 8 (10:10) times, 1 tr in same ch sp as last st, turn. (9 (11:11) 2tr-cl)
ROW 2 (WS) 3 ch, miss first ch sp, *2tr-cl, 1 ch, rep from * across, turn. (8 (10:10) 2tr-cl)
ROW 3 (RS) 3 ch, *2tr-cl, 1 ch, rep from * 7 (9:9) times, 1 tr in same ch sp as last st, turn. (8 (10:10) 2tr-cl)

>> This sweater is made with Louisa Harding Orielle DK, 50g/110m/120yds, in Breeze (05).

ROW 4 (WS) 3 ch, miss first ch sp, *2tr-cl, 1 ch, rep from * across, turn. (7 (9:9) 2tr-cl)

ROW 5 (RS) 3 ch, *2tr-cl, 1 ch, rep from * 6 (8:8) times, 1 tr in same ch sp as last st, turn. (7 (9:9) 2tr-cl)

ROW 6 (WS) 3 ch, miss first ch sp, *2tr-cl, 1 ch, rep from * across, turn. (6 (8:8) 2tr-cl)
Fasten off.

RIGHT SIDE

ROW 1 (RS) Join yarn to 11 (12:14)-ch sp after row end for left side shaping, 3 ch, *2tr-cl, 1 ch, rep from * to end, 1 tr, turn. (9 (11:11) 2tr-cl)

ROW 2 (WS) 3 ch, *2tr-cl, 1 ch, rep from * 7 (9:9) times, 1 tr into turning ch. (8 (10:10) 2tr-cl)

ROW 3 Work row 2 of Upturned V Stitch pattern.

ROW 4 3 ch, *2 tr-cl, 1 ch, rep from * 6 (8:8) times, 1 htr into turning ch, turn. (7 (9:9) 2tr-cl)

ROW 5 Rep row 3.

ROW 6 3 ch, *2tr-cl, 1 ch, rep from * 5 (7:7) times, 1 htr into turning ch, turn. (6 (8:8) 2tr-cl)
Fasten off.

Back

Work as front to row 2 of Shape the armholes. Rep row 2 until piece measures 19.5 (20.5:21.5)cm/7^{1}/$_{2}$ (8:8^{1}/$_{2}$)in from armhole shaping ending on a WS row.

Shape the neck

RIGHT SIDE

ROW 1 (RS) 3 ch, *2tr-cl, 1 ch, rep from * 6(8:8) times, 1 tr in same ch sp as last st, turn. (7 (9:9) 2tr-cl)

ROW 2 (WS) 3 ch, miss first ch sp, *2tr-cl, 1 ch, rep from * across row, turn. (6 (8:8) 2tr-cl)
Fasten off.

Double crochet edging makes the garment tighter around the cuffs and waist for a better fit. Make sure that you keep an eye on the tension so that the cuffs still contain a level of natural elasticity from the yarn.

LEFT SIDE

ROW 1 (RS) Join yarn to 15 (16:18)th 1-ch sp after end of left side shaping, 3 ch, *2tr-cl, 1 ch, rep from * to end, 1 tr, turn. (7 (9:9) 2tr-cl)

ROW 2 (WS) 3 ch, *2tr-cl, 1 ch, rep from * 5 (7:7) times, 1 tr into turning ch. (6 (8:8) 2tr-cl)
Fasten off.

Sleeves (make 2)

Work 68 (72:74) ch.

ROW 1 1 dc in second ch from hook, 1 dc in each ch to end, turn. (67(71:73)sts)

ROW 2 1 ch, 1 dc in each st to end, turn. Rep row 2 a further 7 times.

ROW 10 1 ch, 1 dc, *2 dc in next st, 1 dc, rep from * to end, turn. (100(106:109)sts)

ROW 11 Work row 1 of Upturned V Stitch pattern. (33 (35:36) 2tr-cl)

ROW 12 Work row 2 of Upturned V Stitch pattern.
Rep row 12 until piece measures 37 (38:39) cm/14^{1}/$_{2}$ (15:15^{1}/$_{2}$)in.
Fasten off.

Finishing

Block all pieces to size.
With Front and Back body pieces RS together, seam together along the shoulder seams, using a ss.

Neckline

ROUND 1 Turn work back so RS is facing, join yarn at shoulder seam, 1 ch, work dc evenly around the neckline, front, and back, working into sides of rows where necessary, join with a ss, turn.

ROUND 2 1 ch, 1 dc in each st around, join with a ss, turn.
Rep round 2 a further 2 times.
Fasten off.

Attaching sleeves

With RS together, using safety pins, pin sleeves into place on body armholes, seam together using a ss.

Seam sides

Using a ss, seam together the sides and sleeves. Weave in all ends.

TOP TIP

Crochet more length in the body for a less cropped look.

Child's hoodie

This cosy hooded jacket, for a small person in your life, is worked straight and then seamed. The edging in crab stitch gives a neat detail for a practical jacket.

PROJECTS

For more crab stitch patterns
>> go to pages 72 and 102

Essential information

DIFFICULTY LEVEL Intermediate

SIZE To fit a child, aged 3-4 (4-5:6-7) years

YARN Any 4-ply yarn with a high wool content will produce a similar effect

A x 7(7:8)   **B** x 1(1:2)

CROCHET HOOK 3mm hook

NOTIONS Yarn needle
5 toggles, 3cm (1¼in) long

TENSION 21 sts x 17 rows per 10cm (4in) square

SPECIAL ABBREVIATIONS

1 dc worked at the start of a row counts as a dc stitch.
3 dc worked at the start of a row counts as a tr stitch.
CRAB STITCH: See p.102

Pattern

The first size given is for a small hoodie, with the medium and large sizes in brackets.

Back

With yarn B, work 68 (72:76) ch.
FOUNDATION ROW Starting in the third ch from hook, work 1 dc into each st to end. Break off yarn B and join yarn A. (67(71:75)sts)
ROW 1 Work 3 ch (for the first tr), work 1 tr into each st to end.
ROW 2 Work 1 ch, work 1 dc into each st to end.
These two rows form the pattern.
Repeat these rows until the piece measures 20 (24:28)cm/8 (9½:11)in from beginning, ending with a row 2.

Shape for armholes

Keep pattern correct throughout.
NEXT ROW 1 ch, work 1 ss into each of the first 4 (5:6) st of the row. 3 ch (for first tr), work 1 tr into each stitch to the last 3 (4:5) sts, turn.

Neat wooden toggles look appropriate for this hoodie and finish it off with a lovely detail. They are easier for small hands to do up, although buttons can be substituted if preferred.

(61(63:65)sts)
Keeping pattern correct, work straight until the piece measures 13.5 (15:16.5)cm/ 5½ (6:6½)in from armhole.

Shape shoulders and neck

NEXT ROW 1 ch, work 1 ss into each of the next 9 (9:8) sts, work 1 dc into each of the next 9 sts, work 1 ss into each of the next 25 (27:31) sts, work 1 dc into each of the next 9 sts, work 1 ss into each of the last 9 (9:8) sts.
Fasten off yarn.

Left front

With yarn B, work 34 (36:38) ch.
FOUNDATION ROW Starting in the third ch from hook, work 1 dc into each st to end. (33(35:37)sts)
Break off yarn B and join yarn A.
ROW 1 Work 3 ch (for the first tr), work 1 tr into each st to end.
ROW 2 1 ch, 1 dc into each st to end.

The contrasting pale-coloured edging around the hem, hood, and sleeves gives this hoodie a professional and neat finish. Turn to pages 30–33 when working the increase and decrease stitches to shape the garment, and pages 51–52 for further details about edgings and finishings on crocheted items.

Repeat these rows until the piece measures 20 (24:28)cm/8 (9^1/$_2$:11)in from beginning, ending with a row 2.

Shape for armholes

Keep pattern correct throughout.
NEXT ROW (RS) 1 ch, work 1 ss into each of the first 4 (5:6) st of the row. 3 ch (for first tr), work 1 tr into each stitch to end. (30(31:32)sts)
Keeping pattern correct, work straight until the piece is 6 rows shorter than the back (not including the shoulder shaping row) ending on a WS row.

Shape neck

NEXT ROW 3 ch (for first tr), work 1 tr into each st until 9 (9:11) sts to end, turn. (21(22:21)sts)
NEXT ROW 3 ch (for first tr), tr2tog, work 1 tr into each st to end. (20(21:20)sts)
NEXT ROW 3 ch (for first tr), work 1 tr into each st to the last 2 sts, tr2tog. (19(20:19)sts)
NEXT ROW 3 ch (for first tr), tr2tog, work 1 tr into each st to end. (18(19:18)sts)
Work 2 rows straight.

Shape shoulder

NEXT ROW (RS) 1 ch, work 1 ss into each of the next 8 (9:8) sts, work 1 dc into each of the st to end. Fasten off yarn.

Right front

Make as per left front, but reverse the shaping.

Sleeves (make 2)

With yarn B, work 30 (32:35) ch.
FOUNDATION ROW Starting in the third ch from hook, work 1 dc into each st to end. (29(31:34) sts)
Break off yarn B and join yarn A.
ROW 1 Work 3 ch (for the first tr), work 1 tr into each st to end.
ROW 2 Work 1 ch, work 1 dc into each st to end.
ROW 3 Work 3 ch (for the first tr), work 2 tr into next st, work 1 tr into each st to last 3 sts, work 2 tr into next st, 1 tr into the last st. (31(33:36)sts)

ROW 4 Work 1 ch, work 1 dc into each st to end.
ROW 5 Work 3 ch (for the first tr), work 1 tr into each st to end.
ROW 6 Work 1 ch, work 2 dc into next st, work 1 dc into each st to last 2 sts, work 2 dc into next st, work 1 dc into last st. (33 (35:38)sts)
Continue in this way, increasing every third row, until there are 53 (61:66) sts.
Work straight until the sleeve measures 26 (30:34)cm)/10^1/$_4$ (12:13^1/$_2$)in.
Fasten off yarn.

Pockets (make 2)

With yarn A, work 19 (23:25) ch.
FOUNDATION ROW Starting in the third ch from hook, work 1 dc into each st to end. (18(22:24)sts)
Working in patt as for back, work 13 rows.
ROW 14 1 ch, work 1 ss into each of the next 3 sts, work 1 dc into each st to end. (15(19:21)sts)
ROW 15 3 ch (for first tr), work 1 tr into each st to end.
ROW 16 1 ch, work 1 ss into each of the next 2 sts, work 1 dc into each st to end. (13(17:19)sts)
ROWS 17–21 Work in patt, decreasing 1 st at the shaped edge (by working 2 sts together) on each row. (9(13:16)sts)
Work 2 rows straight.
Fasten off yarn.
Block all pieces.

Buttonhole band

ROW 1 Join yarn A to the top of the left front and work 1 ch. Work in dc along the front edge, working 2 sts into each tr row end and 1 dc into each dc row end. Do not work into the contrast colour at the base of the front.
ROW 2 Work 1 ch, work 1 dc into each st to end.
Repeat row 2 once more.
ROW 3 As row 2 but placing 5 buttonholes evenly along the row. Buttonholes are created by working 2 ch and missing 2 sts.
Repeat row 2 twice more.
Fasten off yarn.

Button band

Starting at the base of the right front, work as for the buttonhole band, replacing row 3 with another row 2 repetition.
Join the shoulder seams.

Hood

With yarn A, starting at the top of the right front button band, work dc around the neck as follows: 5 across the button band, 17 (18:20) sts around the right neck, 25 (27:31) sts across the back neck, 17 (18:20) sts around the left neck, 5 across the buttonhole band. (69(73:81)sts)
Work in patt as for back until the hood measures 24 (26:28)cm/9^1/$_2$ (10:11)in.
Fasten off yarn. Sew top of hood.

Edgings

SLEEVES

Join yarn B to cuff and work in crab stitch along base.
Fasten off yarn.

POCKETS

ROW 1 Join yarn B and work 1 ch. Work 15 dc evenly across the shaped edge.
ROW 2 1 ch, work in crab stitch back across the edging.
Fasten off yarn.

BODY OF JACKET

ROW 1 Join yarn B to the base of the buttonhole band, where it joins the main jacket, and work in dc as follows: base of buttonhole band 5 sts, body and hood, 2 sts into each tr row end and 1 st into each dc row end, base of button band 5 sts.
ROW 2 1 ch, work in crab stitch back across the edging.
Fasten off yarn.
Join sleeves to fronts and back of jacket.
Sew sleeve and side seams; sew pockets to front of jacket; sew toggles to button band.
Weave in all ends.

>> This hoodie is made with Rowan Pure Wool 4-ply, 50g/160m/175yds, in A: Kiss (436) and B: Porcelaine (451).

Summer tunic dress

This sweet, summer tunic dress is worked in two pieces for the front and back, which are then seamed together. The skirt is worked in the round from the top down, using increases and decreases to create a chevron effect.

PROJECTS
For more chevron patterns
>> go to page 80

Essential information

DIFFICULTY LEVEL Intermediate

SIZE To fit a child, aged 1-2 (2-3:4-5) years

YARN You can use any DK weight cotton yarn to achieve a similar effect

A x 2 (2:3)   **B** x 1   **C** x 1   **D** x 1

E x 1   **F** x 1

CROCHET HOOK 3.5mm hook

NOTIONS Yarn needle
2 x 2cm (³⁄₄in) buttons

TENSION 17 sts x 12 rows per 10cm (4in)

Pattern

With yarn A, work 51 (55:59) ch.
ROW 1 1 htr in second ch from hook, 1 htr in each ch to end, turn. (49(53:57)sts)
ROW 2 2 ch, 1 htr in each st to end, turn.
ROW 3 2 ch, 2 (4:2) htr, *1 ch, miss 1 st, 3 htr, rep from * to last 3 sts, 1 ch, miss 1 st, 2 (4:2) htr.

ROW 4 2 ch, 1 htr in each st and ch sp as you come to them, turn.
Rep row 2, 1 (2:3) times.

Shape underarm
ROW 1 Ss into next 3 sts, 3 ch, 43 (47:51) htr, turn. (43(47:51)sts)
ROW 2 2 ch, 1 htr, htr2tog, htr to 3sts from end of row, htr2tog, 1 htr, turn. (41(45:49)sts)
Rep row 2, five times. (31(35:39)sts)
ROW 8 2 ch, 1 htr in each st to end.
Rep row 8 until piece measures 6 (6:7)cm /2¹⁄₄ (2¹⁄₄:2³⁄₄)in from underarm shaping.

Shape neckline
LEFT SIDE
ROW 1 2 ch, 9 (10:11) htr, turn.
ROW 2 2 ch, miss next st, 1 htr in each st to end, turn. (8(9:10)sts)
ROW 3 2 ch, htr in each st to end, turn.
Rep last 2 rows a further 2 (3:4) times. (6sts)
Fasten off.

RIGHT SIDE
ROW 1 Join yarn with ss to 13 (15:17)th st from edge of left side shaping, 2 ch, 1 htr in each st across, turn. (9(10:11)sts)
ROW 2 2 ch, 1 htr in each st to last 2 sts, miss next st, 1 htr. (8(9:10)sts)
ROW 3 2 ch, 1 htr in each st to end, turn.
Rep last 2 rows a further 2(3:4) times. (6sts)
Fasten off.

Back
Work as front to end of first row 2.
ROW 3 2 ch, 1 htr, *1 ch, miss 1 st, 3 htr, rep from * to end.

Continue as front from first row 4 to row 8 of underarm shaping.
Rep row 8 until piece measures 11 (12:14)cm /4¹⁄₂ (5:5¹⁄₂)in from underarm shaping.

Shape neckline
RIGHT SIDE
ROW 1 2 ch, 6 htr, turn.
Rep row 1 a further 3 times.
ROW 4 2 ch, 2 htr, htr2tog, 2 htr, turn. (5sts)
ROW 5 (BUTTONHOLE) 2 ch, 2 htr, 1 ch, miss next st, 2 htr, turn.
ROW 6 2 ch, 2 htr, htr in ch sp, 2 htr, turn.
ROW 7 1 ch, 1 htr in each st to end, turn.
Rep row 7 once. Fasten off.

LEFT SIDE
Join yarn with ss to 19 (23:27)th st from edge of right shaping.
Work as right side.

Join front and back panels
With RS facing, using ss, seam tog side seams under arm holes on both sides.

Skirt
With RS facing, join yarn A at the right side seam.
ROUND 1 2 ch, 2 htr in next st, 1 htr in each st to left seam, 2 htr in next st, 1 htr in each st to end of round. (96(104:112)sts)
ROUND 2 With yarn B, 3 ch (counts as a st), 1 tr in same st as ch 3, *1 tr, (tr2tog) twice, 1 tr, (2 tr in next st)** twice, rep from * to end of round, ending last rep at **, join to top of first st with ss.
Rep round 2.

With yarn A, rep round 2.

ROUND 5 With yarn C, 3 ch, 2 tr in same st as ch 3, *1 tr, (tr2tog) twice, 1 tr, (3 tr in next st)** twice, rep from * to end of round, ending last rep at **, join. (120(130:140)sts)

ROUND 6 3 ch, 1 tr in same st as ch 3, *2 tr, (tr2tog) twice, 2 tr, (2 tr in next st)** twice, rep from * to end, ending last rep at **, join.

ROUND 7 With yarn A, rep round 6.

ROUNDS 8–9 With yarn D, rep round 6.

ROUND 10 With yarn A, rep round 6.

ROUNDS 11–12 With yarn E, rep round 6.

ROUND 13 With yarn A, 3 ch, 2 tr in same st as ch 3, *2 tr, (tr2tog) twice, 2 tr, (3 tr in next st)** twice, rep form * to end of round, ending last rep at **, join. (144(156:168)sts)

ROUND 14 With yarn F, 3 ch, 1 tr in same st as ch-3, *3 tr, (tr2tog) twice, 3 tr, (2 tr in next st)** twice, rep from * to end, ending last rep at **, join.

ROUND 15 Rep round 14.

ROUND 16 With yarn A, rep round 14.

ROUND 17 With yarn B, rep round 14.

SIZES 2–3 AND 4–5 YEARS ONLY

ROUND 18 Rep round 14.

SIZE 4–5 YEARS ONLY

ROUND 19 With yarn A, rep round 14.

ROUNDS 20–21 With yarn C, rep round 14.

ALL SIZES Fasten off.

Finishing

With yarn E, join to right underarm side seam, 1 ch, evenly work a round of dc all the way around the edge of the top, front, and back, join. Fasten off.

Tie

With yarn F, work 150 ch, fasten off, weave in ends. Thread tie through eyelets in row 3 of bodice and fasten with a bow at the front. Weave in ends. Sew buttons in place. Block lightly.

>> This dress is made with Debbie Bliss Eco Baby, 50g/125m/137yds, in A: Ecru (16), B: Corn (36), C: Silver (30), D: Apple (06), E: Fuchsia (32), and F: Aqua (05).

Straw beach bag

The base of this eye-catching yet practical bag is worked in rows, and then the rest of the bag is worked in the round, to the desired height.

PROJECTS

For more half treble patterns
>> go to page 114

Essential information

DIFFICULTY LEVEL Easy

SIZE 32 x 56cm (12½ x 22in)

YARN Any 4-ply weight, durable yarn (held double) such as cotton, linen, or string will work

A x 7   **B** x 6

CROCHET HOOK 5mm hook

NOTIONS Yarn needle
2cm (¾in) button

TENSION Exact tension is not essential

NOTE 2 ch at the beginning of each htr row or round is classed as the first st worked in the first st of previous row.
1 ch at the beginning of each dc row or round is classed as the first st worked in the first st of previous row.
Hold yarn double for extra strength.

Pattern

FOUNDATION ROW With yarn A, work 47 ch.

ROW 1 Htr in third ch from hook and in each ch across, turn. (46sts)

ROW 2 2 ch, htr in each stitch across, turn. (46sts)

ROWS 3–11 Repeat row 2.
Now working in rounds.

ROUND 1 1 ch, dc in each st to end of row, 2 dc in each row end, 1 dc in back of each foundation ch, 2 dc in each row end, join with a ss. (136sts)

ROUND 2 2 ch, htr in each st around, join with a ss.

ROUNDS 3–16 Repeat round 2.

ROUNDS 17–28 With yarn B, repeat round 2.

Handles

ROUND 29 2 ch, htr in next 12 sts, 60 ch, miss next 20 sts, htr in next 48 sts, 60 ch, miss next 20 sts, htr in next 35 sts, join with a ss.

ROUND 30 Htr in each stitch and ch around, join with a ss.

ROUNDS 31–32 Htr in each stitch around. Fasten off.

Fastening flap

With yarn B, work 11 ch.

ROW 1 Dc in second ch from hook and in each ch across, turn. (10sts)

ROW 2 1 ch, dc in each st across, turn. (10sts)

This bag has a very sturdy base, achieved by working in straight rows. The hemp yarn used here makes for a summery feel, but for a slightly more rigid bag try using raffia.

ROWS 3–4 Repeat row 2.

ROW 5 1 ch, dc in first 4 sts, 2 ch, miss next 2 sts, dc in last 4 sts, turn.

ROW 6 1 ch, dc in first 4 sts, dc in each of the 2 chs, dc in last 4 sts, turn.

ROWS 7–20 Repeat row 2.
Dc evenly around entire flap to neaten.
Fasten off. Sew flap and button onto bag.

>> This bag is made with Expressions hand-coloured hemp, 4-ply, 50g/85m/93yds, in A: Wow (orange) and B: Yippi (green).

Super-stretchy shopper

This handy bag is made in the round with a solid base and a mesh body. Worked in double crochet, the fabric is strong and flexible, and so the bag will expand to fit lots of shopping inside.

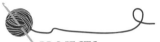

PROJECTS

For more double crochet patterns
>> go to page 70

Essential information

DIFFICULTY LEVEL Easy

SIZE Approx 25.5 x 33cm (10 x 13in), with 48.5cm (19in) handles

YARN You can use any DK cotton or cotton mix yarn here to get a similar effect

x 5

CROCHET HOOK 4.5mm

NOTIONS Stitch marker
Yarn needle

TENSION Exact tension is not essential

NOTE Mark the first stitch of each round.

Pattern

Work 2 ch.

ROUND 1 8 dc in second chain from hook.

ROUND 2 2 dc in first st, and in each st around. (16 dc). Do not join with a ss. Continue to work in a spiral, remembering to mark the first st of each round.

ROUND 3 *2 dc in next st, 1 dc in next st, rep from * around. (24sts)

ROUND 4 *2 dc in next st, 1 dc in next 2 sts, rep from * around. (32sts)

ROUND 5 *2 dc in next st, 1 dc in next 3 sts, rep from * around. (40sts)

ROUND 6 *2 dc in next st, 1 dc in next 4 sts, rep from * around. (48sts)

ROUND 7 *2 dc in next st, 1 dc in next 5 sts, rep from * around. (56sts)

ROUND 8 *2 dc in next st, 1 dc in next 6 sts, rep from * around. (64sts)

ROUND 9 *2 dc in next st, 1 dc in next 7 sts, rep from * around. (72sts)

ROUND 10 *2 dc in next st, 1 dc in next 8 sts, rep from * around. (80sts)

ROUND 11 *2 dc in next st, 1 dc in next 9 sts, rep from * around. (88sts)

ROUND 12 *2 dc in next st, 1 dc in next 10 sts, rep from * around. (96sts)

ROUND 13 *2 dc in next st, 1 dc in next 11 sts, rep from * around. (104sts)

ROUND 14 *2 dc in next st, 1 dc in next 12 sts, rep from * around. (112sts)

ROUND 15 *2 dc in next st, 1 dc in next 13 sts, rep from * around. (120sts)

ROUND 16 *2 dc in next st, 1 dc in next 14 sts, rep from * around. (128sts)

ROUND 17 *2 dc in next st, 1 dc in next 15 sts, rep from * around. (136sts)

ROUND 18 *2 dc in next st, 1 dc in next 16 sts, rep from * around. (144sts)

ROUND 19 Dc in each st around.

ROUNDS 20–23 Repeat round 19.

Mesh rounds

Now mark the first 4-ch sp at the beginning of each round.

ROUND 24 *4 ch, miss 2 sts, dc in next, rep from * around, ending with a 4 ch.

ROUND 25 Dc in first 4-ch sp, *4 ch, dc in next 4-ch sp, rep from * around, ending with a 4 ch.

ROUNDS 26–65 Repeat round 25.

ROUND 66 Dc in next dc (mark this stitch), * 2 dc in next 4-ch sp, dc in next st, rep from * around.

ROUND 67 Dc in first st (mark this stitch), and in each st around.

ROUNDS 68–70 Repeat round 67. Fasten off.

Handles (make 2)

Work 13 ch.

ROW 1 Dc in second chain from hook and in each ch across, turn. (12sts)

ROW 2 1 ch, dc in each st across, turn. (12sts)

ROWS 3–46 Repeat row 2. Fasten off.
Sew the handles on the bag and weave in ends.

>> This bag is made with Rowan Softknit Cotton, 50g/105m/115yds, in Sunset red (582).

Crocheting in the round is easy to achieve and allows you to be more versatile with your stitching.

Hanging toy basket

This pretty accessory will be at home in any child's playroom. Constructed in spirals using double crochet, it can easily be tackled by a beginner. Instructions are given for a medium and large toy basket.

PROJECTS

For more spiral patterns
>> go to page 70

Essential information

DIFFICULTY LEVEL Easy

SIZE 25 (30) x 40 (45)cm/9¾ (12) x 15¾ (17¾)in

YARN Any aran weight or cotton blend could be used here

A x 2   **B** x 1   **C** x 1

CROCHET HOOK 3.5mm hook

NOTIONS Stitch marker
Yarn needle

TENSION 14 sts x 16 rows per 10cm (4in)

NOTE Worked in the round in a spiral, do not turn and do not join at end of each round.

Pattern

With yarn A, ch 4 and join with a ss to form a ring.

ROUND 1 1 ch (does not count as stitch), 6 dc into ring, place marker to indicate last st of round (move marker up at end of each round, so it always indicates last st). (6sts)

ROUND 2 2 dc into each st. (12sts)

ROUND 3 *1 dc in next st, 2 dc in next st, rep from * to end. (18sts)

ROUND 4 *1 dc in next 2 sts, 2 dc in next st, rep from * to end. (24sts)

ROUND 5 *1 dc in next 3 sts, 2 dc in next st, rep from * to end. (30sts)

ROUND 6 *1 dc in next 4 sts, 2 dc in next st, rep from * to end. (36sts)

ROUND 7 *1 dc in next 5 sts, 2 dc in next st, rep from * to end. (42sts)

ROUND 8 *1 dc in next 6 sts, 2 dc in next st, rep from * to end. (48sts)

ROUND 9 *1 dc in next 7 sts, 2 dc in next st, rep from * to end. (54sts)

ROUND 10 *1 dc in next 8 sts, 2 dc in next st, rep from * to end. (60sts)

ROUND 11 *1 dc in next 9 sts, 2 dc in next st, rep from * to end. (66sts)

ROUND 12 *1 dc in next 10 sts, 2 dc in next st, rep from * to end. (72sts)

ROUND 13 *1 dc in next 11 sts, 2 dc in next st, rep from * to end. (78sts)

ROUND 14 *1 dc in next 12 sts, 2 dc in next st, rep from * to end. (84sts)

ROUND 15 *1 dc in next 13 sts, 2 dc in next st, rep from * to end. (90sts)

ROUND 16 *1 dc in next 14 sts, 2 dc in next st, rep from * to end. (96sts)

LARGE SIZE ONLY

NEXT ROUND *1 dc in next 15 sts, 2 dc in next dc, rep from * to end. (102sts)

Continue without shaping until piece measures 16cm (6¼in) for small size and 18cm (7in) for large size from round 1.

LARGE SIZE ONLY

NEXT ROUND *1 dc in next 15 sts, dc2tog, rep from * to end. (96sts)

BOTH SIZES

NEXT ROUND *1 dc in next 14 sts, dc2tog, rep from * to end. (90sts)

NEXT ROUND *1 dc in next 13 sts, dc2tog, rep from * to end. (84sts)

NEXT ROUND *1 dc in next 12 sts, dc2tog, rep from * to end. (78sts)

NEXT ROUND *1 dc in next 11 sts, dc2tog, rep from * to end. (72sts)

Change to B and work 6 (8) rounds in dc as set.
Change to C and work 2 (2) rounds in dc as set.

Hanging loop

At start of next round, make 20 ch, miss 12 sts, dc to end of round. (60sts and 20ch)

NEXT ROUND 1 dc in each ch and 1 dc in each st to end of round. (80sts)

Work 4 (5) rounds in dc as set.

FINAL ROUND 1 ss in each dc to end.

Fasten off yarn, weave in ends. Block lightly according to instructions on ballband.

>> This hanging toy basket is made with Sirdar Simply Recycled Aran, 50g/93m/102yds, in A: Turq (38), B: Lime (39), and C: Coral (37).

Essential information

DIFFICULTY LEVEL Intermediate

SIZE Approx 28 x 16cm (11 x 6¼in)

YARN You can use any DK weight yarn

A x 1   **B** x 1

CROCHET HOOK 3.75mm hook

NOTIONS 2 stitch markers
Yarn needle
12mm (½in) black safety toy eyes
Brown embroidery thread and needle
Brown felt for inner ears
Toy stuffing
1cm-wide velvet ribbon

TENSION Exact tension is not essential

SPECIAL ABBREVIATIONS
ADJUSTABLE RING: Wind the yarn twice around
your finger. Insert the hook and wrap the yarn
around it. Pull the hook back through and work
a chain. Work the first round of sts into the "ring",
then pull the tail of yarn gently to close it, before
joining the sts into a round using a ss.

Teddy bear

You never forget your first bear and this one is sure to become a true keepsake. Worked in the round using adjustable rings for neatly curved paws and feet, this project is quick and satisfying to make.

PROJECTS
For more toy patterns
>> go to pages 125

NOTE The teddy bear is worked in spirals. Do not join rounds, but place a marker at first stitch of the round, moving it each round to mark the beginning of the next round.

Pattern
Follow this pattern and then refer to page 55 when assembling your toy.

Head
With yarn A, make an adjustable ring and work 6 dc into the ring. (6sts)
ROUND 1 2 dc into each st to the end. (12sts)
ROUND 2 *1 dc, 2 dc in the next st; rep from * to end. (18sts)
ROUND 3 *2 dc, 2 dc in the next st; rep from * to end. (24sts)
ROUND 4 *3 dc, 2 dc in the next st; rep from * to end. (30sts)
ROUND 5 *9 dc, 2 dc in the next st; rep from * to end. (33sts)
ROUND 6 *10 dc, 2 dc in the next st; rep from * to end. (36sts)
ROUND 7 *11 dc, 2 dc in the next st; rep from * to end. (39sts)

<< This bear is made with Rico Design Essential Cotton DK, 50g/130m/142yds, in A: Brown (081) and B: Beige (09).

ROUND 8 *12 dc, 2 dc in the next st; rep from * to end. (42sts)
ROUND 9 *13 dc, 2 dc in the next st; rep from * to end. (45sts)
Place 2 stitch markers on the next row 10 sts apart to mark where you will put the toy eyes.
ROUND 10 *14 dc, 2 dc in next st; rep from * to end. (48sts)
ROUND 11 *15 dc, 2 dc in next st; rep from * to end. (51sts)
ROUND 12 *16 dc, 2 dc in next st; rep from * to end. (54sts)
ROUNDS 13–14 Dc in each st to end.
ROUND 15 *dc2tog, 7 dc; rep from * to end. (48sts)
ROUND 16 *dc2tog, 6 dc; rep from * to end. (42sts)
ROUND 17 *dc2tog, 5 dc; rep from * to end. (36sts)
ROUND 18 *dc2tog, 4 dc; rep from * to end. (30sts)
ROUND 19 *dc2tog, 3 dc; rep from * to end. (24sts)
ROUND 20 *dc2tog, 2 dc; rep from * to end. (18sts)
ROUND 21 *dc2tog, 1 dc; rep from * to end. (12sts)
Add some stuffing to the head now.
ROUND 22 *dc2tog; rep from* to end. (6sts)
Put the working loop on a stitch holder and attach the toy eyes to the head in the places you marked on round 10.
Finish stuffing the head. Weave the cut yarn through the last 6 sts, pull to close the hole at the base of the head. Weave in yarn to secure and cut off any loose ends.

Muzzle
With yarn B, make an adjustable ring and work 6 dc into the ring. (6sts)
ROUND 1 2 dc into each st to end. (12sts)
ROUND 2 *3 dc, 2 dc in the next st; rep from * to end. (15sts)
ROUND 3 Dc in each st to end.
ROUND 4 *4 dc, 2 dc in next st; rep from * to end. (18sts)
ROUNDS 5–6 Dc in each st to end.
ROUND 7 *5 dc, 2 dc in next st; rep from * to end. (21sts)
ROUND 8 Dc in each st to end.
Cut the yarn leaving a long tail and pull through loop to secure.
Position the muzzle carefully and sew it onto the face. Use brown embroidery thread to sew the nose and mouth detail on the muzzle. Weave in and cut off any loose ends.

Body
With yarn A, make an adjustable ring and work 6 dc into the ring. (6sts)
ROUND 1 2 dc into each st to end. (12sts)
ROUND 2 *3 dc, 2 dc in next st; rep from * to end. (15sts)
ROUND 3 *4 dc, 2 dc in next st; rep from * to end. (18sts)
ROUND 4 Dc in each st to end.
ROUND 5 *5 dc, 2 dc in next st; rep from * to end. (21sts)
ROUND 6 Dc in each st to end.
ROUND 7 *6 dc, 2 dc in next st; rep from * to end. (24sts)
ROUND 8 Dc in each st to end.
ROUND 9 *7 dc, 2 dc in next st; rep from * to end. (27sts)

The legs are worked from the feet upwards. Start with an adjustable ring (see p.27) and maintain even tension as you increase the number of stitches on each round. Stuff the legs as they evolve.

ROUND 10 Dc in each st to end.
Add some stuffing to the body now.
ROUND 11 *8 dc, 2 dc in next st; rep from * to end. (30sts)
ROUND 12 Dc in each st to end.
ROUND 13 *9 dc, 2 dc in next st; rep from * to end. (33sts)
ROUND 14 Dc in each st to end.
ROUND 15 *10 dc, 2 dc in next st; rep from * to end. (36sts)
ROUND 16 Dc in each st to end.
ROUND 17 *dc2tog, 10 dc; rep from * to end. (33sts)
ROUND 18 *dc2tog, 9 dc; rep from * to end. (30sts)
ROUND 19 *dc2tog, 3 dc; rep from * to end. (24sts)
ROUND 20 *dc2tog, 2 dc; rep from * to end. (18sts)
ROUND 21 *dc2tog, 1 dc; rep from * to end. (12sts)
ROUND 22 *dc2tog; rep from * to end. (6sts)
Cut the yarn leaving a long tail and pull through loop to secure. Finish stuffing the body. Thread the cut yarn onto a yarn needle and weave through the last 6 stitches, pull the

yarn to close the hole at the top of the body. Sew the body firmly to the head. Weave in and cut off any loose ends.

Arms (make 2)

Stuff the arms as you go along.
With yarn A, make an adjustable ring and work 6 dc into the ring. (6sts)
ROUND 1 2 dc into each st to end. (12sts)
ROUND 2 *1 dc, 2 dc in the next st; rep from * to end. (18sts)
ROUND 3 *2 dc, 2 dc in the next st; rep from * to end. (24sts)
ROUNDS 4–6 Dc in each st to the end.
ROUND 7 *dc2tog, 2 dc; rep from * to end. (18sts)
ROUND 8 *dc2tog, 4 dc; rep from * to end. (15sts)
ROUND 9 *dc2tog, 3 dc; rep from * to end. (12sts)
ROUNDS 10–19 Dc in each st to end.
ROUND 20 Dc2tog, dc in each st to end. (11sts)
ROUNDS 21–25 Dc in each st to end.
ROUND 26 Dc2tog, dc in each st to end. (10sts)
ROUNDS 27–28 Dc in each st to end.
Cut the yarn leaving a long tail and pull through loop to secure.
Finish stuffing the arm firmly.
Thread the cut yarn onto a wool needle and weave through the last 10 stitches, pull the yarn to close the hole at the top of the arm, weave in yarn to secure.
Position the arms carefully in place and sew them onto the body.

Legs (make 2)

Stuff the legs as you go along.
With yarn A, make an adjustable ring and work 6 dc into the ring. (6sts)
ROUND 1 2 dc into each st to end. (12sts)
ROUND 2 2 dc, 2 dc in the next st, 2 dc, 3 htr in the next st, 2 htr, 3 htr in the next st, 2 dc, 2 dc in the last st. (18sts)
ROUND 3 3 dc, 2 dc in the next st, 2 dc, 1 htr, 2 htr in the next st, 4 htr, 2 htr in the next st, 1 htr, 1 dc, 2 dc in the next st, 2 dc. (22sts)
ROUND 4 2 dc in the first st, 8 dc, 3 htr in the next st, 5 htr, 3 htr in the next st, 6 dc. (27sts)

ROUND 5 Dc in each st to end.
ROUND 6 1 dc, dc2tog, 8 dc, dc2tog, 6 dc, dc2tog, 6 dc. (24sts)
ROUND 7 11 dc, htr3tog, 3 htr, htr3tog, 4 dc. (20sts)
ROUND 8 3 dc, dc2tog, 4 dc, dc2tog, 1 dc, dc2tog, 1 dc, dc2tog, 3 dc. (16sts)
ROUND 9 8 dc, dc2tog, 1 dc, dc2tog, 3 dc. (14sts)
ROUND 10 Dc in each st to end.
ROUND 11 Dc2tog, dc in each st to end. (13sts)
ROUNDS 12–16 Dc in each st to end.
ROUND 17 Dc2tog, dc in each st to end. (12sts)
ROUNDS 18–22 Dc in each st to end.
ROUND 23 Dc2tog, dc in each st to end. (11sts)
ROUNDS 24–28 Dc in each st to end.
ROUND 29 Dc2tog, dc in each st to end. (10sts)
Cut the yarn leaving a long tail and pull through loop to secure.
Finish stuffing the legs firmly.
Thread the cut yarn onto a wool needle and weave through the last 10 stitches, pull the yarn to close the hole at the top of the leg, weave in yarn to secure. Position the legs carefully and sew onto the body.

Ears (make 2)

With yarn A, make an adjustable ring and work 6 dc into the ring. (6sts)
ROUND 1 2 dc into each st to end. (12sts)
ROUND 2 *1 dc, 2 dc in next st; rep from * to end. (18sts)
ROUND 3 Dc in each st to end.
ROUND 4 *2 dc, 2 dc in next st; rep from * to end. (24sts)
ROUND 5 Dc in each st to end.
ROUND 6 *3 dc, 2 dc in next st; rep from * to end. (30sts)
ROUNDS 7–8 Dc in each st to end.
ROUND 9 Dc2tog, dc in each st to end. (29sts)
ROUND 10 Dc2tog, dc in each st to end. (28sts)
Cut the yarn, leaving a long tail, and secure.
Cut two pieces of felt and stitch them inside the ears using running stitch. Try not to allow the stitches to go through to the outer ear. Sew the ears onto the head. Weave in and cut off any loose ends. Tie a velvet ribbon around the bear's neck.

Animal rattles

These bright and colourful rattles will delight any young baby. The double crochet stitch makes the toy robust and durable for lots of cheerful play. Change the character of each rattle by choosing a different animal's face.

PROJECTS

For another toy pattern
>> turn to pages 122-124

Essential information

DIFFICULTY LEVEL Intermediate

SIZE 12cm (5in)

YARN You can use any DK weight cotton yarn for a similar effect

A x 1   B x 1   C x 1   D x 1   E x 1

CROCHET HOOK 3mm hook

NOTIONS Stitch marker
Yarn needle
Black and pink embroidery thread and needle
Toy stuffing
Soft toy bell (to place inside the rattle)

TENSION Exact tension is not essential

SPECIAL ABBREVIATIONS
ADJUSTABLE RING: See p.122

NOTE Work in continuous spirals unless pattern states otherwise. Mark the end of the round with a st marker, and move it up as you work.

Dog rattle

ROUND 1 With yarn A, make an adjustable ring with 6 dc. (6sts)
ROUND 2 2 dc into each st. (12sts)
ROUND 3 *1 dc, work 2 dc into next st; rep from * around. (18sts)
ROUND 4 *2 dc, work 2 dc into next st; rep from * around. (24sts)
ROUND 5 *3 dc, work 2 dc into next st; rep from * around. (30sts)
ROUNDS 6–9 Dc around. (30sts)
ROUND 10 *3 dc, dc2tog; rep from * around. (24sts)
ROUND 11 *2 dc, dc2tog; rep from * around. (18sts)
ROUNDS 12–14 With yarn B, dc around. (18sts)
ROUNDS 15–17 With yarn C, dc around. (18sts)
ROUNDS 18–20 With yarn B, dc around. (18sts)
ROUNDS 21–23 With yarn C, dc around. (18sts)
ROUNDS 24–26 With yarn B, dc around. (18sts)
ROUND 27 With yarn A, *2 dc, work 2 dc into next st; rep from * around. (24sts)
ROUND 28 *3 dc, work 2 dc into next st; rep from * around. (30sts)
ROUNDS 29–32 Dc around. (30sts)
ROUND 33 *3 dc, dc2tog; rep from * around. (24sts)

Place a small bell in the base of the rattle and stuff the rattle firmly before continuing with the crochet.
ROUND 34 *2 dc, dc2tog); rep from * around. (18sts)
ROUND 35 *1 dc, dc2tog; rep from *around. (12sts)
ROUND 36 *dc2tog; rep from * around. (6sts)
Using a yarn needle gather the last 6 sts together. Fasten off, weave in ends.

Ears (make 2)

ROUND 1 With yarn A, make an adjustable ring with 4 dc. (4sts)
ROUND 2 2 dc into each st. (8sts)
ROUNDS 3–4 Dc around. (8sts)
ROUND 5 *2 dc, dc2tog; rep from * around. (6sts)
ROUNDS 6–7 Dc around. (6sts)
Ss to join. Fasten off, weave in ends.

Finishing

Sew ears firmly to either side of rattle head. Embroider nose and eyes with black thread.

Maintain a tight tension for a firm fabric that hides the stuffing.

TOP
TIP

The mouse's ears are made from two different-coloured pieces of crocheted fabric. Once both are complete, place the shapes wrong sides together and work a series of double crochet stitches in the head colour around them both to create the edging.

Keep your tension even when working each round. This will ensure a firm, close-knit fabric. To stuff each rattle, push the toy stuffing gently with your index finger to the base of the animal, then complete the design by crocheting its head and ears.

Each animal's eyes, nose, and mouth are sewn with six strands of black and pink embroidery thread. Bend the earflap of the dog downwards and secure it with a small stitch from underneath the ear to the side of the dog's head.

Cat rattle

Repeat main pattern for rattle, replacing the colours with C, D, and B in that sequence.

Ears (make 2)

ROUND 1 With yarn C, make an adjustable ring with 4 dc. (4sts)

ROUND 2 1 dc, work 2 dc into next st); rep. (6sts)

ROUND 3 (2 dc, work 2 dc into next st); rep. (8sts)

Ss to join and fasten off. Weave in ends.

Finishing

Sew ears firmly to either side of rattle head. Embroider nose, whiskers, and eyes with black yarn.

Mouse rattle

Repeat main pattern for rattle, replacing the colours with D, E, and A in that sequence.

Ear front (make 2)

ROUND 1 With yarn A, make an adjustable ring with 8 dc. (8sts)

ROUND 2 Work 2 dc into each st. (16sts)

ROUND 3 (1 dc, work 2 dc into next st); rep around. (24sts)

Ss to join and fasten off. Weave in ends.

Ear back (make 2)

ROUND 1 With yarn D, make an adjustable ring with 8 dc. (8sts)

ROUND 2 Work 2 dc into each st. (16sts)

ROUND 3 (1 dc, work 2 dc into next st); rep around. (24sts)

Ss to join and fasten off. Weave in ends.

Finishing

Take one ear front and ear back and place wrong sides together, using yarn D and with the ear front facing, dc both sides of the ear together. Ss to join and fasten off, weave in ends. Sew ears firmly to either side of rattle head. Embroider nose with pink thread and whiskers and eyes with black thread.

>> These rattles are made with Rico Design Essential Cotton DK, 50g/130m/142yds, in A: Pistachio (86), B: Banana (63), C: Magenta (13), D: Light blue (27), and E: Nature (51).

Dorling Kindersley would like to thank the following people for their hard work and contributions towards *Crochet*:

Crochet designers

Lesley Arnold-Hopkins: Child's hat with earflaps p.88, Tweed stitch cowl p.96, Child's hoodie p.111; **Vicki Brown:** Men's chunky socks p.104, Ladies' ankle socks p.106, Cropped sweater p.108, Summer tunic dress p.114; **Simone Francis:** Intarsia cushion p.110; **Melanie Galloway:** Straw beach bag p.76; **Helen Jordan:** Broomstick shawl p.92; **Claire Montgomerie:** Beaded necklace p.58, Party bunting p.62, Flower garland p.64, Structured baskets p.66, Flower pin cushion p.68, Fruit bowl p.72, Circular cushion p.78, Chevron cushion p.80, Mobile phone covers p.82, Coin purses p.84, Baby bonnet p.86, Ladies' wrist warmers p.94; **Irene Strange:** Baby boy's booties p.100, Baby girl's booties p.102; **Tracey Todhunter:** Striped washcloths p.60, Rustic pouffes p.70, Chunky rug p.74, Child's mittens with string p.98, Hanging toy basket p.120.; **Emma Varnam:** Woman's beret p.90, Baby rattles p.125; **Liz Ward:** Teddy Bear p.122.

Yarn manufacturers and distributors who supplied yarn for projects:

Artesano Ltd, Coats Craft UK, Designer Yarns Ltd, DMC Creative World, King Cole Ltd, Rico Design, Sirdar Spinning Ltd, Texere Yarns Ltd, Thomas B. Ramsden & Co. 2014 Crochet: Senior Editors May Corfield, Katharine Goddard, Dorothy Kikon; Senior Art Editor Glenda Fisher, Zaurin Thoidingjam, Neha Wahi; Photography Ruth Jenkinson; Art Director/Stylist for Photography Isabel de Cordova; Pattern checker Carol Ibbetson; Photography assistant Julie Stewart; Props Backgrounds Prop Hire; Location for photography 1st Option ; Models Estelle Abberley, Georgia Abberley, Celia Arn, Liz Boyd, Joshua Caulfield, Maria Clancy, Claire Cross, Maria Elston, Marco Elston, Lucas Goldstein, Saskia Janssen, Martha Jenkinson, Bodhi Nair, Tulsi Nair, Clara Proctor, Martha Rhodes, Julie Stewart, Eden White, Mia White, and Oscar the cat

Claire Montgomerie is a textiles designer who specializes in crochet and knitting, constructing fabrics, garments, creatures and accessories that are fun, quirky and modern. Her main aim is to reinvent the products of ancient and traditional needlecraft processes, while retaining all their intricacies and comforting charm. Claire has written many crochet and knitting books and also edits the UK craft magazine, *Inside Crochet*.